D0411235

Visiting Distilleries

Visiting Distilleries

DUNCAN & WENDY GRAHAM

www.visitingdistilleries.com

ANGELS'SHARE ®

is an imprint of
Neil Wilson Publishing Ltd
303a The Pentagon Centre
36 Washington Street
GLASGOW
G3 8AZ

Tel: 0141-221-1117
Fax: 0141-221-5363
E-mail: info@nwp.sol.co.uk
http://www.nwp.co.uk

© Duncan and Wendy Graham, 2001

The authors have asserted their moral right under the
Design, Patents and Copyright Act, 1988, to be identified
as the Authors of this Work.

Picture credits: p90, Seagram Distillers; p108, SMWS; p110, SWHC.
All other pictures were taken by the authors.
Cover picture of Lagavulin Distillery by Robbie Porteous.
Illustrations on pages 4-9 were prepared by Doreen Shaw.
All the maps were prepared by Robert Burns.

A catalogue record for this book is available from the British Library.

ISBN 1-903238-09-9
Typeset in Frutiger and Aldine
Designed by Robbie Porteous
Printed in China

Contents

Introduction

It all started with Queen Victoria. On the 12th September, 1848, she dropped in on Lochnagar Distillery on Deeside with her consort, Prince Albert, and unwittingly started the business of visiting distilleries.

Well, perhaps not, but we should give credit where credit is due. After that visit Lochnagar became 'Royal' and the cellars at Buckingham Palace began to take in large stocks of that distillery's product. (She was also keen on a dram in her afternoon cuppa!) But the floodgates didn't exactly open after her visit. Even after Alfred Barnard's historic tour of the whisky distilleries of the United Kingdom in 1886, in which he detailed his travels to 129 distilleries in Scotland, 28 in Ireland and four in England, visiting distilleries was literally unheard of.

Any distillery at that time would have been a strictly functional affair with no provision for visitors, and it wasn't until the 1960s that the industry began to exploit its malt whisky distilleries by marketing them as visitor attractions. Not only was the popularity of single bottled malt Scotch on the increase by then, but also the realisation that many distilleries were ideal visitor attractions because they served as places of pilgrimage for the faithful and initiation for those new to the growing cult. Most of them also happened to be situated in some of Scotland's most glorious scenery.

Our personal inspiration for this book came from the many visits we have made to whisky distilleries over a number of years. We are only two of the million or so people who undertake this increasingly popular pastime every year. During these visits we were able to form lots of impressions as to how visitors are dealt with by the distillery owners. Not all of these impressions were favourable and at times we were struck by a lack of information on what to expect, and by the quality of the experiences which lie beyond the ubiquitous 'Visitors Welcome' sign.

The quality and scope of the tour, the range of things to see and experience, the facilities available – varying from 'there is a public loo along the seafront' to a state-of-the-art visitor centre, the access for disabled visitors, and the warmth of the welcome (or lack of it) – all of these factors set us thinking that others might welcome a book of this type. In *Visiting Distilleries* our aim is to offer the kind of advice and information we felt we could have done with, together with simple guidelines as to what to expect, and the kind of questions (and answers) which can make the whole distillery visit worthwhile. And if any of you are asking, 'But all distilleries are the same, aren't they?', believe us – they are not!

Friends often ask us, 'Where on earth do you start?' Which distilleries are beginner-friendly? Which ones within a given region are ideal for the children on a wet August afternoon? Which ones could be logistically strung together in a smaller or larger tour? And folk who know much more about whisky than we shall ever know, have asked us where to go to see something specific to add to their already considerable experience. In this book, we have tried to answer these questions.

On planning this venture we accepted that there was no ideal way of gathering the information. Advance information gathered from distillers was all very well, but the acid test was to visit all those distilleries (and a few other related facilities) open to visitors within a period of time short enough to allow us to fairly compare and identify the features folk ask about. In our house we have a tradition that no bottle of malt should remain unopened after it has been purchased. We are not 'collectors' in that respect. We can offer visitors their pick of 20 to 30 bottles, all of them at varying levels of volume. Like all good ideas, the one behind this book gradually formed during a more extensive investigation of our stocks in the company of our publisher, Neil Wilson, himself no stranger to the joys of the cratur. As that session progressed the logistics of our mission seemed to ease considerably. Reality set in the next day as we pondered again our visit to 40 or more establishments ranging geographically from Orkney to Wigtown, from Skye to Huntly, and all within the space of one Scottish summer.

The next stage was to plan itineraries. In the end we came down to areas which do not correspond with the rather confusing pigeon-holing of the malt whisky industry – how can Glengoyne, with a Glasgow postcode (yet in Stirlingshire) and Glenmorangie in Tain, on the shores of the Dornoch Firth, both meaningfully be 'Highland'? The system we have chosen in this book is the result of some common-sense logistics and the urgent need to find centres from which to foray forth. There are obvious 'hotspots' such as Speyside, with ten distilleries (and a cooperage); Islay and Jura with seven; the far North with eight and the Central Highlands with seven. Elsewhere distances are greater and common factors more difficult to identify. The Islands and the West Coast cover a wide area, but there is a common feeling of remoteness that somehow links them together. The distilleries in the South of Scotland have little in common and are best visited simply when the opportunity arises.

Our travels involved a Fiat motor caravan, a BMW F650GS motorcycle, a Subaru Legacy estate car, sundry ferries and toll bridges, and some rather splendid b&bs. We dined on everything from lobster thermidor in Stromness to pasta salad in the Scotch Whisky Heritage Centre in Edinburgh. Some of the best meals and snacks were enjoyed in distilleries, ranging from the cordon bleu standard at Glenturret, via island home cooking at Ardbeg, to sandwiches from Eaglesomes, the grocers owned by Springbank, eaten on the seafront at Campbeltown. The sun shone most of the time (honestly), and the welcomes we experienced were invariably a credit to Scottish hospitality. The malt whisky business, despite commercial rivalries, is a fairly close-knit family with a degree of dedication which other industries might usefully emulate. Sadly, we found very, very, few people who expressed much sympathy for the ordeal to which we had subjected ourselves!

When we embarked on our expedition, we were not experts on whisky and its distillation. We have however learned a fair amount, and have certainly widened our range of preferred drams. It has frequently been said that, 'There are no bad whiskies, some are just less good!' To that we would add that nearly everything is down to personal preference, or the mood and ambience of the moment. We have given you our personal views and those of some experts on the whiskies we sampled. On everything else, the opinions are our own – close enough to your needs, we hope, to help you and informed enough to give valid opinions. In future editions we hope to meld and moderate our views in the light of your experiences. To that end do take time to fill in and send us the Visitor Response Form (or photocopy it) at the end of the book, or log on to the Visiting Distilleries website at www.visitingdistilleries.com and fill out the form online.

Every effort has been made to ensure accuracy in factual details, and to be as up-to-date as possible. If you are in any in doubt, please check with each distillery visitor centre – some of the quieter ones can be closed completely for the 'silent season'. Some errors are bound to have crept in and we apologise for them in advance. The views expressed are honestly held, based on our own experience and reliable advice from fellow enthusiasts. Enjoy Visiting Distilleries.

Duncan and Wendy Graham, Appleby, Cumbria

How Malt Whisky is Made

Malt whisky is made from three major ingredients: water, yeast and barley. The fourth ingredient is the people who make it. It is their skill and craftsmanship, passed down from generation to generation, which makes it what it is.

The processes that create malt whisky can be broken down into three main areas: brewing, distillation and maturation. In the first instance the barley has its energy-rich starch content converted to soluble sugars (by malting). These sugars are then extracted (by mashing in hot water) and after the addition of yeast, a weak alcoholic brew called wash is produced (fermentation). This is then distilled and the resultant spirit is stored in oak casks for at least three years in order to be called Scotch whisky.

Brewing

Malting: In order to prepare the barley for malting, it is first steeped in water cisterns for around 48 hours and, after draining, the sodden grains are allowed a period of time to germinate as the starches are converted. This can be seen on malting floors such as at Laphroaig, where the 'piece' (as the blanket of barley is known) will lie for seven days, or in larger drum maltings which exist on an industrial scale, such as at Port Ellen (also on Islay) and at Ord. Malting takes around six days to complete at Port Ellen. At present Golden Promise, Optic and Prism varieties are popular malting barleys.

During germination the rootlets must be kept disentangled and the grain conditioned by turning the 'piece'. On a typical malting floor some 25 tonnes of barley can be turned manually or by tractor to achieve this while in a maltings plant such as Port Ellen, the rotation of the drums has the same effect. When the barley is in prime condition the maximum amount of starch conversion has taken place and, in order to preserve these sugars, germination must be stopped. This is achieved by drying the barley, now known as 'green malt'.

Kilning: There are two ways to kiln green malt. The traditional way is in a pagoda kiln, but it is more likely to be done in an industrial maltings prior to delivery to the distillery. Few distilleries which still kiln their barley can satisfy their total needs, and the greater proportion of barley required is supplied from industrial maltings.

In a traditional kiln, the green malt is spread on a mesh floor above a furnace. The drying effect of the heat and the smoke from burning peat help create the phenolic content of the barley which in turn affects the flavour of the whisky.

Nowadays, malts vary in phenolic content and flavour from zero (such as Glengoyne) to very high (Ardbeg, with over 50 parts per million). The required level of phenols is achieved by varying the proportion of primary and secondary fuels used for drying. For instance, at Bowmore the primary fuel is actually recycled heat from the distillation process, with a precise amount of macerated peat added to raise the phenols to the specified level. At Springbank, the complex and phenolic Longrow is produced by spending some 55 hours over peat, while the medium-peated Springbank only spends six hours over peat and 18 over the oil-fired heat source. The malt for the peat-free Hazelburn (due in 2007) is dried exclusively over an oil-fired heat source.

After the kilning is over, the malted barley is stored in elevators or silos to await milling.

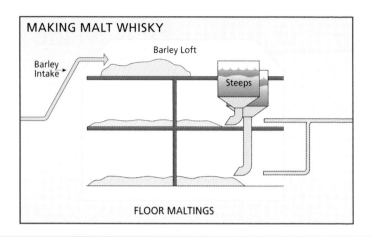

MAKING MALT WHISKY

Barley Loft

Barley Intake

Steeps

FLOOR MALTINGS

What to look out for

Distilleries with Maltings

At Bowmore, Laphroaig, Highland Park and Springbank (and perhaps at Glendronach in the future) – look out for the steeps, the malting floors, the tools for turning the piece and the pagoda-roofed kilns. Peer into the furnaces if full of peat, and try to smell the reek in the kilns when the fires are out and access is possible. It is well worth the effort to see a malting floor and kiln in action.

Everywhere else

Look for clues from the past – disused kilns, malting floors (often now converted to retail use and visitor centres) and the tell-tale pagodas. But beware: some of these are modern facsimiles (Isle of Arran). Former malting floors often have regular smallish windows on two or three floors to effect the correct degree of ventilation and temperature control. A good example of this is Benromach.

The distillery guides should show visitors where malted barley is unloaded and stored and also indicate where it has come from.

Milling: To make sure that the maximum amount of soluble sugar is extracted, the malted grains are now crushed and milled. As the rollers in the mills are susceptible to damage, the malt must be dressed to remove dust and husks before being passed through a destoner. Even after malting a kilo or two of stones can always be rattled out of each lorry load. The malt is then passed over magnets where metallic oddments are fielded. Then down into the mill – traditionally made by Porteous of Hull and Leeds, or Boby of Bury St Edmunds. Usually maroon in colour, and often venerable in age, the mills can be noisy and dusty in action, but visitors should be able to view them in action (except in Arran where all the grain comes ready-milled). The milling must be carried out in such a way as to produce a consistency which will not congeal and clog up the mashtun during the next stage. For that reason the 'grist', as the milled malt is known, must contain just the right proportion of husk along with coarse and fine floury material. The millman will test for this using a wooden box-like apparatus, containing sieves of varying mesh size, so that a sample can be graded to show the required proportions. A load for a single mashing can take over an hour to mill.

What to look out for

- The destoners and dressers which are often on a higher level than the mill. The wooden conveyors and the box of grading sieves.

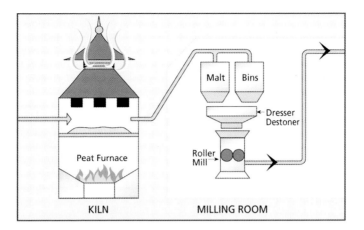

Inside the diagram:

Malt | Bins

← Dresser Destoner

Roller Mill

Peat Furnace

KILN   MILLING ROOM

- Is it a Porteous or a Boby mill? How old is it? What colour is it? Are there fresh samples of the constituents of grist to see and feel?
- If you haven't seen the malting process, look out for samples of newly malted barley – they should be fresh enough to taste and enjoy.
- How does the grist get from the milling room to the mashtun?

Mashing: The mashtun is really a huge teapot. The grist is infused with hot water drawn from tanks known as 'coppers' and then mixed by the submerged stirring apparatus. The resultant brew is a sugar-rich liquid called 'wort'. After the first mashing, a large proportion of the sugars will have been dissolved and the wort is drained off through the perforated sieve floor into the underback. Three or four infusions take place using increasingly hot water ranging from 65°c to 93°c. The run-off, excepting the last lot of weak, sugary water, also passes to the underback. The last water is added to the first hot water for the next mash. Successive 'mashes' provide more of the sugary liquid wort which then fills the washbacks for fermentation.

After the wort has been extracted, the spent grains and husks are called 'draff' (or 'wet grains' in Ireland) – and this bran is extracted from the mashtun (actually by shovel at Edradour, in the old-fashioned way) and carted off as premium cattle food.

Most distilleries have one mashtun, and some have two. The majority are made of stainless steel, with a few made of cast-iron sections with flanged edges riveted together like the Forth Railway Bridge. Ardbeg has a modern steel tun skinned with the old iron originals and most of them have lids or canopies that range from prosaic steel to glorious copper with hatches trimmed in brass. Inside every mashtun there is either a lautering mechanism or a series of stirring arms arranged around a vertical, central axis, driven from outside the tun. Some of these look a little like a Heath-Robinson device, but are great fun to see in action with their cogged wheels running on tracks inside the perimeter of the mashtun.

What to look out for

- Relative sizes of mashtuns. From quite small at Glenturret and Arran, to huge at Tomatin or Bunnahabhain.
- What is the mashtun made of? Stainless steel or cast iron? Has it a steel or a copper canopy – or none at all?
- Can you find a maker's plate with date of manufacture?
- What kind of agitator mechanism does it have?

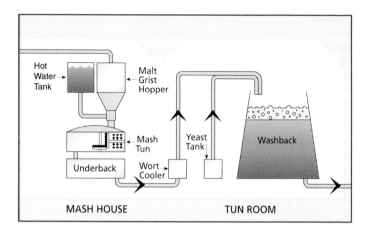

| MASH HOUSE | TUN ROOM |

(Diagram labels: Hot Water Tank, Malt Grist Hopper, Mash Tun, Yeast Tank, Washback, Underback, Wort Cooler)

- How is the grist delivered and the wort extracted – is there a connecting underback full of wort to be seen close by?
- What happens to the draff? At Dalmore it exits through pipes cleaned by firing a size-5 football through them!

Fermentation: First, the wort has to be cooled, otherwise it destroys the yeast. The wort is passed through a cooler which may vary from those which look like milk coolers as seen in farm dairies (Edradour), through some that resemble old bull-nose Morris car radiators, to smart blue and grey Alfa–Lavals (Clynelish), made of space-age materials. The wort is then passed into one of up to eight (or even 16) washbacks and the yeast is then added. This can be distiller's yeast, brewer's yeast, or a mix of the two. It can be introduced as a liquid or tossed straight in from dry sacks, as at Strathisla.

What to look out for

- The yeast store. This might be a dry store or a refrigerated plant. Is there an open pre-mix yeast tank? When this is bubbling away, it is worth seeing: the strange strawberry aroma merit sampling.
- How does the yeast get into the washbacks?

The washbacks: In the early days of distilling fermentation used to be carried out in wooden barrels which might explain why most washbacks today are, in effect, huge barrel a dozen feet (3.65m plus) or more across, and often 20 feet (6m) deep. Knot-free wood is required which used to mean Scottish larch, but more often nowadays means Oregon pine Some distilleries use stainless steel washbacks, which are easier to clean and are more hygienic However, the jury is out on whether fermentation in stainless steel alters the end-produc more than 48 to 72 hours fermentation in traditional wood. What is beyond doubt is how unromantic, cold and bleak stainless steel washbacks look when compared to warm, multi hued, stained and worn wooden backs with their striking red, green or black steel hoops Nowadays guides at Glenmorangie, otherwise so beautiful a place, quickly hustle visitors pas an aesthetic desert of steel washbacks reminiscent of a hospital laundry.

Because the washbacks are gradually filled, in sequence, with wort from the mashtun, the all operate at different stages of fermentation. At its peak, fermentation is a violent process – washbacks simmer with life, and the foaming head can reach up to the top of the backs. I 'switchers' (lazily turning froth beaters) are not used to break up the head, or if staff ignor

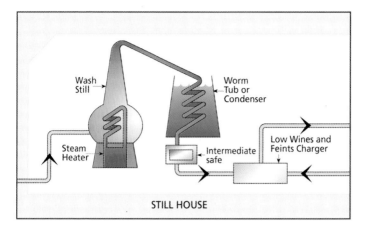

it, it can force its way past the heavy, wooden lids. Guides should show visitors the process at various stages, and allow visitors to cup a hand into the top of the back and scoop out a heady draught of carbon dioxide. But do not dip your head right in or you'll feel that you have been punched in the face! Early on in the process, the contents taste of sugar, but by the latter stages (after around 40 hours), they have become a dirty, brown, foaming liquid which is bitter and almost beer-like. The proper name for this is 'wash' and it is sometimes called 'weak beer'. At 7-8% abv, however, it carries a substantial kick and few are tempted to try it!

What to look out for

- How old are the washbacks and what are they made of?
- Can you estimate their depth? Often the floors are open, wire, grid plates and some distilleries install lights below this level.
- How does fermentation progress? Can you guess what stage it is at? How can you tell when a washback is on the 'way up' or the 'way down'?
- Above all, look, sniff, and savour.
- How is the wash transferred to the stillroom for the next stage?

Distillation

If the mash room is the 'tearoom' of the distillery, and the washbacks the 'brewery', then surely the stillroom is the 'cathedral'. Nothing quickens the pulse of the visitor, casual and aficionado alike, more than the sight of gleaming, curvaceous copper stills. Here is the very source of the mystique, the inner temple of the cult of malt. No two distilleries are identical in their stills, each one maintaining subtle and not-so-subtle traditional patterns in both their spirit and wash stills. But why are there two types of still?

The reason is that Scotch malt whisky is usually distilled twice (rarely thrice and occasionally two-and-a-half times, as at Springbank). Stills are normally steam heated through internal coils, or, in a few cases, directly coal-fired, as at Glenfiddich. The wash enters the wash still first where a robust distillation occurs due to the presence of yeast residue and other impurities. Normally there is a window high up the neck through which the stillman can see if the distilling wash is about to boil over and allow liquid rather than vapour to cascade over the top.

The vapours which rise up the neck fall over into the 'lyne arm' (which may be broad or

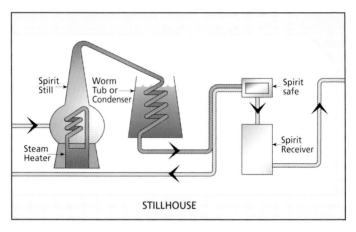

STILLHOUSE

narrow, horizontal or even up-sloping); then into the condensers where they become liquid with an alcoholic strength of 21% to 23% abv. This is stored as 'low wines' – having passed through an intermediate spirit safe for the first time. From there the low wines are charged into the spirit still (or stills) for a second distillation. What is left in the wash still is called 'pot ale' and is disposed of as cattle food, often mixed with draff to form cattle cake.

During the second distillation in the spirit (low wines) still, the initial run of spirit is known as the 'foreshots' and is diverted to the low wines and feints charger. The middle cut is retained and flows into the spirit receiver. (The foreshots are re-distilled with the next charging of the spirit still.) The middle cut is determined by the stillman when a strength of spirit of 67-68 % abv (dependent on temperature) is reached and he checks for this in the spirit safe. As the strength tails off, he again diverts the end of the distillation (known as 'feints') to the low wines and feints charger for re-distillation. His timing has to be spot on to achieve quality and consistency in selecting the middle cut.

The sticky residue left in the spirit still is called the 'spent lees' and is the only waste by-product of the entire distilling process.

What to look out for

- Relative size of stills. Tall, as on Jura or petite as at Edradour. Slender at Glenmorangie, or chunky at Pulteney – or anything in between. They may be 'double-onion' or even sport a 'mini-onion' – in short anything goes and each extravagance is alleged to add character and uniqueness. Tall narrow stills are claimed only to allow the lighter spirits to pass over and hence produce a lighter malt – such as Glen Grant or Glenkinchie. In such stills, the heavier spirit falls back (or 'refluxes') to 'go round again'. Copper is sacrificial and wears, but stills are seldom replaced in their entirety – just in case the magic is lost. They are in reality a 'thing of shreds and patches' and at one time patches were obvious as they were riveted in: nowadays welding by experts such as Forsyth of Rothes is more discreet and barely visible. If the stills are not in use, peer inside to see the coiled heating pipes. A rummager might be visible in the wash still. This is the heavy chain which churns round the inside of the base to prevent the heavy impurities sticking to the bottom and burning solid. Once this was a nasty cleaning job for a man with a brush made of twigs and heather.
- The condensers. Most of these are copper-clad cylinders sitting behind the stills and connected directly to the lyne arm. Occasionally they are outside if the stillroom is small. At Bowmore there are three inside and one outside due to lack of space. A few distilleries have worm condensers with the cooling alcoholic vapour passing through copper pipes set in vast tubs of water – as was once the way of illicit and farm stills.

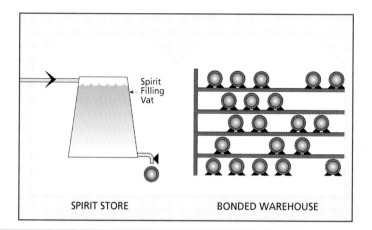

SPIRIT STORE   BONDED WAREHOUSE

Dalwhinnie and Talisker are good examples of this, with their worm tubs clearly visible outside the stillroom walls.

- The spirit safe (or safes): Look out for the maker's name – often a clue as to who made the stills and the mashtun as well. Many stills date from the 1960s, and Ardbeg replaced a 50-year old still in 2000. The names become like old friends after a few visits. Many of these firms are out of business – the main contractor now is the aforementioned Forsyth of Rothes.

- The spirit receivers. Cold steel or warm oak – the latter surely a kinder introduction for the spirit to the years in the barrel.

Maturation

Casking: Sometimes, as at Aberfeldy, most of the spirit is poured unglamorously into tanker-lorries and whisked off to mature elsewhere before blending. A true malt whisky should be casked and warehoused on site. Visitors should be able to see casks being filled, wooden bungs (usually elm) being driven home, and the cask ends stencilled with the date, cask number, name of the distillery and owner of the contents.

What to look out for

- Casks of varying sizes, stencils for marking (often now accompanied by the omnipresent and distinctly utilitarian barcode) how leaks are detected, and the skills of barrel-manipulation. The master of the cask is undoubtedly Ian MacArthur at Lagavulin – a star in his own right on home videos from Kansas to Kirkcaldy.

Maturation: Hardly action packed, but this is the part of the process which most influences the end-product. Raw, newly distilled spirit is colourless and harsh, and far removed from its final glory. It is the combination of breathing in cask and absorbing the soluble constituents of the wood that, with the passage of time, works its magic. Nowadays most whisky is matured in casks of American oak which have served one four-year stint maturing bourbon. Such casks are often bought by whisky distillers before use in Kentucky and after being broken down into staves, are brought over in flatpacks and reassembled in Scotland. At Glenmorangie an expert actually selects trees in the Ozark Mountains for their casks – it is that crucial for the company.

The other mainstay is the use of ex-sherry casks. The tight-grained wood of these Spanish oak casks imparts a darker colour and often more than a hint of sherry sweetness. The best bottled malts frequently result from a mix of whiskies matured in sherry and bourbon casks together with some second or third refill whisky casks. Balance is achieved by 'marrying' the contents of the chosen casks before bottling. (Macallan is the place to see how the casks are selected after a careful 'nosing'.)

By law new spirit must mature for a minimum period of three years in duty-free warehouses before it can legally be called Scotch whisky. The length of further maturation depends on what sort of whisky the distiller wants in its eventual bottled form. Various factors affect this, such as the initial characteristics of the whisky when distilled, the local microclimate, the size of the cask, and whether the cask is fresh or was previously used for bourbon or sherry (or even wine, port and Madeira). The average maturation time is 10-12 years. Because of evaporation – the loss of 2% of volume per year, also known as the angels' share – the longer a whisky is matured, the less is left in the cask and the more it tends to cost. After the optimum period, it can become too 'woody'. Maturation is halted when a whisky is bottled – unlike wine, laying it down does not improve the quality or the flavour.

What to look out for

- The different sizes of American and European casks. These range from 175 to 500 litres (38-110 gallons) – barrels, hogsheads, butts and puncheons. Oak trees mature for 100-150 years before use and oak is the only wood that prevents seepage while allowing the contents to 'breathe'.

- The style of warehouse – old-fashioned dunnage warehouses are most interesting – pressed earthen floors, thick walls, casks stacked only two or three racks high. Modern warehouses may use steel racks up to eleven layers high – can they be as perfect as the traditional ones? With expanding production they are inevitable – even Macallan swear by them and aver that temperature and atmosphere controls match the best dunnage bonds.

- The exciseman's office – a glass-partitioned area strategically placed just inside the door of the spirit filling store or in the bonds where a steely-eyed official once watched every move made by the warehousemen – not always successfully. Sometimes they themselves were corrupted by temptations too exquisite to resist. (A lifelike model exciseman with a gimlet eye looks the part at Tomatin).

- The stencils and the tales they tell.

- One-off 'celebrity' casks.

- Port, Madeira and wine casks being used for 'finishing' the fashionable double-matured whiskies.

Above all, glory in the atmosphere, the odours, smells and aromas – the only and most sublime way to savour the angels' share.

Bottling: In Scotland this is only carried out on the premises at Springbank, where visitors cannot view it, and at Glenfiddich, where they can. This is a sight not to be missed there – serried ranks of bottles proceeding in an orderly manner to filling, corking, labelling and packing. In Ireland, Bushmills is the place to witness this. Otherwise it is a case of transporting tanker lorries of whisky to bottling plants (usually in Central Scotland) which then complete the job.

A Brief History of Scotch

As mentioned in the previous chapter, whisky is elemental, consisting of three ingredients: water, yeast and barley. The procedure by which alcohol is created from these ingredients is simple too.

It can be split into three main parts: brewing (mashing and fermentation) and distilling which is then followed by the process which has the greatest effect on the whisky which arrives in the bottle – maturation.

Hundreds of years ago the process was essentially the same as that witnessed in today's distilleries, the only real difference being that maturation was not a consideration then – once whisky was distilled, it was not long before it was consumed. In those days, the action of wind-blown yeasts on moistened cereal grains would have accidentally created a barley 'bree', essentially a precursor to beer. Once the production of beer was mastered, the craft of distillation, imported from the Orient by monks and crusaders, would have taken the process to its next stage and created alcohol. Farmers and crofters were well placed to master these crafts as they had all the raw materials to hand.

The word alcohol derives from the Arabic *al-koh'l* which surprisingly seems to have been a form of mascara. As to how it is connected to drink, we can only surmise, but the mind boggles with the possibilities! The Egyptian males, well versed in brewing and distilling, do seem to have enjoyed making themselves up, but perhaps they needed a little fortification before doing so. Who knows?

But in time climate must have played its part in the making of alcohol as those dwelling in hotter climes concentrated on the grape, and thence wine, while those enjoying more bracing weather in Northern Europe were forced to use cereals and spirits. The first mention of 'aqua vitae' – the water of life – in Scotland occurs in 1494 but this would mean that the existence of distilled spirit must have stretched back much further. Like so much of the Scots' culture, the knowledge probably was derived from Ireland where there are records of distilleries in the 12th century. In Scotland we know that in 1505 the Guild of Surgeon Barbers of Edinburgh had been given a monopoly of distillation 'for medicinal purposes'– where have we heard that one before!

We do know that by the 17th century in Scotland home distillation was relatively commonplace and was carried out on farms and crofts wherever there were ready supplies of barley and peat for firing a kiln and heating the still. Soaked barley would be spread out on the floor of an outhouse to germinate. As it did so, the starch held within the grains would convert into sugars and to preserve these, the grain would then be spread over a 'haircloth' suspended above an open peat fire in a kiln. Once dry, it would be ground to a coarse 'grist' and then immersed in hot water to make a brewer's porridge. After adding yeast, perhaps supplied by a local baker, fermentation commenced and in due course a weak alcoholic wash' would be produced. After draining the liquor off, it would be charged into a small still atop an oven-like furnace. The alcohol which was boiled off would then run through the condensing worm which sprouted from the top of the still. This coiled into a barrel of cold water beside the still and created the condensate which exited from the bottom. This clear spirit was 'aqua vitae'.

Essentially you can see the same process today, but on a much vaster scale, at Dalwhinnie Distillery. Examples of farm-size stills – of 20 to 50 gallons – are also on view in the museum at Glenkinchie. In time the farmers must have noted that spirit stored in wooden casks improved with age, but there was little reason the keep the whisky back from the market place for this reason.

It has been said that the only sure things in life are death and taxes. While raw liquor can hasten the former, governments can assure the latter. The 17th century saw the inevitable introduction of taxation of alcohol together with clumsy and bitterly resented attempts at enforcement. A 'war' began which has gone on to this day – who can be absolutely sure that illicit distilling is not going on as we write this?

The history of the next 300 years is peppered with tales of gaugers and excisemen, of smugglers and runners. Stills that were hidden in hills, caves and bothies were hunted down and destroyed by day and night by the exciseman and his posse. Frequently the stills were back in business in the next glen straight after the miscreant had paid his dues. Further lore was to come much later with Prohibition and the 'speakeasy' in the United States. The phrase the 'real McCoy' was first used by smugglers working out of Nassau in the Bahamas when the USA created an insatiable demand for good liquor.★ Even today a potent sense of injustice can be felt abroad when travelling Scots find their dram costs more at home than practically anywhere else in the world.

The Union of the Parliaments in 1707 led to redoubled interest in revenue-raising from both brewing and distilling on both sides of the Border. The malt tax riots in Glasgow in 1725 were typical of the feeling of the mob at that time. During those riots Daniel Campbell of Shawfield was compensated to the tune of £9,000 by the city for damage to his mansion in Glassford Street. He used the money to buy a large portion of Islay and Jura and so unwittingly secured the future of distilling on the island. His agrarian reforms were to allow the evolution of distilling on Islay to continue unabated. Illicit stills in the Highlands flourished in spite of the excisemen's best efforts and the spirit from these Highland stills was of a far higher quality than the coarse Lowland distillations carried out in huge, industrial flash-fired stills. This quality spirit came to be called 'usky' from the Gaelic 'uisge' meaning water. In time this became our word 'whisky'. It was a byword for quality.

At the turn of the 18th century, the government was saddled with the Napoleonic War. To pay for it, it became increasingly interested in regulating the spirits industry in order to maximise revenue. Ultimately, illicit distilling had to be harnessed and brought on board in order to achieve this aim. Both 'sides' began to see that more constructive legislation was needed as increasing demand continued unabated. Efforts to eradicate illicit distilling had done little to diminish it; by 1814 only one parish in Argyll did not boast an illicit still. The message was clear.

The turning point came with the Excise Act of 1823 which provided for the licensing of distilleries in much the same way as they are licensed today. It simply made more sense to go legal, to operate openly and within the law and to pay duty according to the regulations. Many of today's Highland distilleries were established at this time, growing from known sites of illicit distillation and thus preserving their farming roots well into the present century. The padlocked spirit safe which visitors see in every distillery dates from this time, as did the presence of on-site excisemen which lasted until the Thatcher government's self-regulation laws in the 1980s.

As the British Empire expanded, so did the market for Scotch whisky and it was soon on the road to claiming truly worldwide status. But it was not the famous single malt whiskies we celebrate today that created this, but rather the blended whiskies that were developed in the mid-19th century which combined Highland and Island malts with grain whiskies made by the Lowland distillers. Grain whisky was by this time being made in a continuous process thanks to the invention of the Coffey still around 1830. By 1860 the blending of grain and malt whiskies was commonplace, and could be carried out in bond, duty-free. Railway expansion made transportation to cities and seaports easier and the Speyside malts were considered ideal for blending. The Islays were used to a lesser degree due to their enormous character (as was Talisker) but they were considered essential blending components. This increase in demand for blends created a boom in distillery building towards the end of the century.

At this time the 'Whisky Barons', such as the flamboyant Tommy Dewar and James

★ Captain Bill McCoy ran only the best quality Scotch to the east coast during Prohibition and his wares were soon considered to be the 'real McCoy'.

Buchanan, toured the world on extensive sales campaigns. Blend brands – Dewars, Johnnie Walker, Buchanan and Bells – became household words at home and abroad as overseas agents snapped up the rights to import, advertise and distribute them. Whisky drinkers seldom came across the single malts of the day, although they were available to private account customers and could be sourced for supply in octave casks from the public house gantries in the UK. But most of the 'whisky' sold in the urban drinking dens at the end of the 19th century was of questionable provenance and there were frequent complaints about doctored whisky. After a series of allegations in the national press in 1913, quality control legislation brought about the precise definition of 'Scotch Whisky' – chief amongst them being that it must be distilled in Scotland and matured for a minimum of three years.

Over the early years of the 20th century, heavy duties, temperance pressures and economic depression all took their toll on the industry. The end of Prohibition in the USA in 1933 threw a lifeline to the Scotch whisky industry which was exploited fully. By 1939, five million gallons of Scotch were crossing the Atlantic annually, and 92 distilleries were in production. Then came the Second World War. It was followed by the 'fire water' era – what student of my generation (DG) can recall Red Hackle without the memory bringing a tear to the eye and a burning sensation to the throat?

Since then the constants have been heavy duties – often raised, sometimes held, never lowered, and more recently the corporate amalgamations which are such a marked feature of the business world. These have brought about countless mergers and in turn ownership by American, European, Canadian and Japanese corporate moguls. The process continues even to this day and as I write the Chivas empire is once more on its way from Canadian ownership to French. It is heartening to see that amongst these big battalions the vibrant independents and smaller players still have a part to play – J&G Grant, Gordon & MacPhail and so on.

The one really wonderful and gratifying development has been the rocketing growth in popularity and sales of single malt whiskies. Single bottled malt is the finest distilled spirit in the world and over the last 50 years has come to equal and surpass the finest of cognacs and armagnacs, with the distinctive product of each distillery earning its devoted band of discriminating followers. The trailblazer for this was the effective and imaginative marketing of Glenfiddich in the 1960s and as more and more mature stocks have become available, the choice available has vastly increased, with first Glenmorangie, Glenlivet and then Laphroaig and Lagavulin becoming available in every airport in the world. Special expressions abound now and the latest development is the double-matured bottlings whereby malts spend their final months in port, wine or vintage sherry casks to 'finish' them off.

The growth of the malt sector within the Scotch industry far outstrips the general growth of the industry itself. The interest in the malt sector is also disproportionate to the contribution made by it to the overall profile of the trade. How can such a seemingly tiny part of the trade as a whole engender such incredible feelings of goodwill on a worldwide basis from people of all races and cultures? The answers are worth searching for and perhaps that is a good reason for visiting distilleries, because that is where the story of malt whisky really begins.

There was a time not so long ago when a visit to a distillery could only be arranged with difficulty via the head office. Members of the trade, MPs and visiting dignitaries were the lucky ones who tended to make it through the distillery front gates and be peered at suspiciously by the exciseman. Now 40 distilleries are open to visitors with facilities ranging from simple tours conducted by the workforce, to state-of-the-art visitor centres. You can even visit your very own cask slumbering away in the warehouse at Springbank. This book will tell you what to expect and what to look out for when you cross the magic threshold into a world of 'beautiful factories' where science combines so felicitously with art.

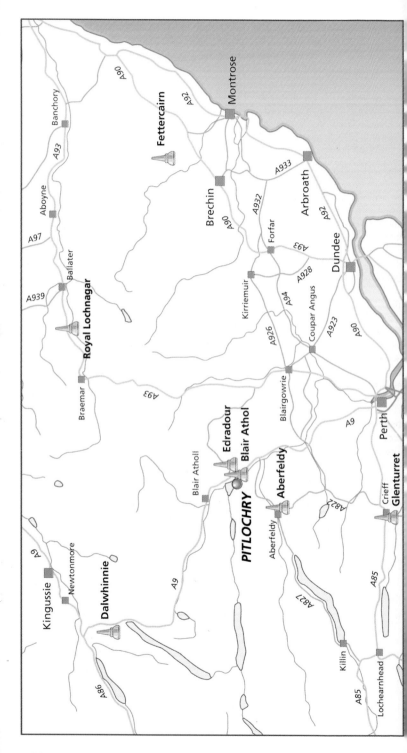

The Central Highlands

There are seven distilleries in this spectacular heartland of Scotland. These are Aberfeldy, Blair Athol (in Pitlochry) Dalwhinnie, Edradour (near Pitlochry), Fettercairn (in the Howe of Mearns) Glenturret (in Crieff) and Royal Lochnagar which is close to Balmoral. All but the last two lie on or near the A9 trunk road from Perth to Inverness. Fettercairn and Royal Lochnagar can be tackled from Pitlochry as part of a very pleasant and beautiful circular tour which embraces Glenshee, Deeside and the stunning Cairn o' Mount (B974). Aberfeldy and Crieff make another nice circular tour going one way by Loch Tay, Killin and Lochearnhead and the other through the Sma' Glen. This provides a perfect pretext to lunch at Glenturret – highly recommended. For those making for the joys of Speyside or the northern distilleries, Dalwhinnie, the highest distillery in Scotland, can be visited en route.

There are many excellent hotels and restaurants and shops in Pitlochry – our favourite retreat is the Moulin Hotel (01796 472196) which lies on the A924 midway between Pitlochry and Edradour. Although a bit off centre the Caravan Club has excellent sites at Braemar and Newtonmore. Milton of Fonab, half-a-mile from Pitlochry, is pleasant too. Bikers (and others) could do a lot worse than the Fortingall, three miles from Aberfeldy (01887 830367) or the Balrobin in Pitlochry (01796 472901).

Other attractions in the Pitlochry area include the salmon ladder and Loch Faskally just north of the town. A gentle drive south on the old road to Dunkeld affords pleasant views of the salmon fishing beats on the Tay and the Tummel. The National Trust cottages in the square at Dunkeld are a delight, while the baker's shop in the main street sells delicious rhubarb and apple tarts in traditional Scottish water pastry. Close by Dunkeld is Birnam Wood where those who know their Shakespeare will recall from Macbeth that these are the same woods that 'walked' to Dunsinane.

ABERFELDY

BLAIR ATHOL

DALWHINNIE

EDRADOUR

FETTERCAIRN

GLENTURRET

ROYAL LOCHNAGAR

ABERFELDY

State-of-the-art 'World of Whisky' exhibition for the young. Quality tour of the distillery for adults.

The distillery stands proud above the road and faces the River Tay. Epitomising the Victorian certainty of the Dewar family, it has a well-proportioned façade in solid grey stone with an imposing pagoda. A modern stillhouse at the end fits in fairly happily. Well-manicured grounds set it off nicely and it's no surprise to learn that red squirrels and even deer can be seen along with rare birds on the adjacent nature trail. The immediate area lacks places to sit and picnic and visitors have limited access to parts of it – even the bit with the restored steam shunter. Still, it's not a bad place to be on a crisp day in January or a showery day in June.

Established 1898

Enquiries 01887 822011

Website www.dewars.com/worldofwhisky

Opening hours 2 Apr-31 Oct, Mon-Sat, 10am-6pm; Sun, 12-4pm; 1 Nov-31 Mar, Mon-Fri, 10am-4pm. Last tour one hour before closing.

Getting there Leave the main A9 five miles south of Pitlochry and join the A827 for Aberfeldy. The distillery cannot be missed on your left just before entering the town. Alternatively take the lovely A826 from Crieff through the 'Sma Glen' and turn right in Aberfeldy.

Parking/reception Parking is up the drive and off to the right – wooden poles mark out the bays. Reception is signposted from the car park as Dewar's 'World of Whisky' entered over a wooden causeway to the first floor of the former maltings, transformed for the millennium into a multi-media exhibition centre. A modern trendy hall with light wood floors, white oak decor and spotlights galore, houses reception, theatre, shop and the 'World of Whisky' experience.

Tour frequency As required.

Maximum group size 20.

Cost £3.95.

Group bookings By appointment with the centre manager.

Visual aids Everything known to science in the exhibition area. Hand-held audio guides, headphones, touch-screen interactives, video quizzes and an e-mail booth – the lot. Leave the kids there while you do the distillery tour which is reassuringly traditional.

Foreign visitors Some audio-visuals in French, German, Spanish (Japanese pending).

Photography in distillery? No

Disabled access? To 'World of Whisky' it is excellent but not the distillery tour.

THE PRODUCT

Malt Aberfeldy

Owner John Dewar & Sons Ltd

Region Highland (southern)

Ages 12 & 25 years old

Water source The Pitilie Burn

Malting Carried out either at Stirling or in Inverness – middle range for phenols.

Bond Casks and warehouses now in Stirling – a pity. Visitors can see former cask-filling area and barrels through a glass panel.

Casks Ex-sherry, bourbon and refill whisky – up to three cycles.

Bottling In Glasgow.

Experts' opinion Lightly-peated, with a full, ripe nose and overtones of walnut and vanilla. Full, smooth, medium-sweet body, a hint of smoke and malt. Lush, well-rounded finish.

Our dram The hard-sell is of Dewar's White Label blend – we wanted to try the malt! We declined their generous dram of WL and settled for the excellent coffee offered as an alternative.

A game of two halves. The first bit you tackle on your own – a video about the Dewar family, an exhibition about the Dewar family, quizzes about the Dewar family. Tommy Dewar was clearly a 'card', but by the end of this bit you will, I guarantee, never want to see or hear of a Dewar again, but even so, kids will love it. Dewars have, over the years, excelled at the art of advertising and the examples here are compelling and are certainly nostalgic for the wrinklies. The exhibition is well laid out but perhaps just too much on the one theme. Part two of the tour starts with the dram and then a first-class guided tour of the distillery – well organised, lucid, with a lot of features not found else-where. The guides, who may well be from mainland Europe, are competent and well-versed. Distillery staff help them out with tricky questions. The tour covers everything from malting to cooperage in a clear logical and visually attractive manner. After the DIY starter it is pleasant to be shepherded unobtrusively between well-chosen vantage points.

Special features A maroon Porteous mill, a fairly large stainless steel mashtun with a shapely peaked cover and a small underback. Then off to see eight handsome washbacks of light-coloured Siberian larch, encircled by maroon hoops to match the overall decor. Later we were able to view them from below and appreciate how tall they stand. Two unusual features come next – a good close view of the open yeast vessel (note the 'strawberry' aroma) and of the 'engine room' consisting of draff pipes from the mashtun, cooling equipment and a lot of mysterious gubbins, (nearly as impres-sive as the paddle steamer *Waverley*!). The stillroom has huge picture windows, open to the ele-ments in clement weather, and houses four stills, two wash and two spirit. All are tall, bulbous yet elegant. Long, narrow, swan necks pass over your head to the copper condensers behind. Abercrombie of Alloa made them originally, although most of them have been replaced bit-by-bit over the years. In 1972 they manufactured two separate spirit safes – one for the low wines and one for the middle cut of the finished spirit. Nearby is a handsome oak spirit receiver leading to a loading bay for tanker lorries. The cooperage video and display is the final highlight of an all-embracing experience.

Access State-of-the-art to the 'World of Whisky'. The distillery itself has wide stairs, with nice wood-en balustrades and space to move around.

Visual impact Decor is burgundy and cream with splendid brass plates on everything you need to know about. The 'World of Whisky' is a visual treat – especially Dewar's study and the mock blend-ing room.

Range Glamorous woollens and fleeces, table mats, fudge, foods and confectionery. Whisky selection fairly limited – Aberfeldy malt, Dewar's White Label, glasses and mugs.

Style White oak, blue and lemon decor. Curiously low-key in contrast to the hard-sell of Dewar's blends in the 'World of Whisky' experience.

Staff Your tour guides preside, friendly, courteous and not too pushy.

Catering None – plans exist for a restaurant in the disused warehouse area.

Toilets Modern, bright, airy, immaculate. Excellent toilets downstairs in the 'World of Whisky'– with a lift for the disabled. **Parent and baby** – incorporated with toilet for the disabled.

Dewar's 'World of Whisky' was created at great cost in 2000 and boasts up-to-date features explor-ing audio-visual techniques to their limits. It's a subjective thing of course, but while it is exciting, especially for children, it is rather too Dewar-family-orientated, and a bit too 'hard-sell' for those of us who prefer a more relaxed and subtle pitch. Perhaps it's just the generation gap showing. (One of Tommy Dewar's famous aphorisms was, 'We have a great regard for old age when it is bottled.') The distillery tour is unreservedly commended. Well-conducted, it is visually pleasing, full of interest and novel features, a positive delight for the visitor. Pity a 'wee sensation' of the Aberfeldy malt is not an option!

Overall rating

VISITED DEC. 2002
TWICE
MAVIS BERRY 1ST VISIT
JOHN & MARGARET SECOND
BOUGHT WHISKY
TWO BOTTLES

Well-presented with good facilities. Excellent tour and fine cafeteria.

Blair Athol Distillery is in Pitlochry (note the difference in spelling to the town of Blair Atholl which is some miles to the north). Although in the town, it has a pleasant almost rural setting with trees and a river, complete with fish-ladder closeby. Set in well-maintained gardens, the buildings exude a feeling of spaciousness and well-proportioned Scottish architecture. The older buildings are covered with a rich warm Virginia creeper which unbelievably comes from only eight roots. A pleasant place to visit and well worth a stroll after the tour and dram.

Established 1798

Enquiries 01796-482003

Website none

Opening hours Easter-Sep, Mon-Sat, 9am-5pm; Jul-Sep, Sun, 12-5pm; Oct, Mon-Fri, 9am-5pm; Nov-Easter, Mon-Fri, 10am-4pm. Telephone for tour times in the winter. Last tour one hour before closing.

Getting there The distillery is not in Blair Atholl at all but a few miles nearer Perth in Pitlochry. It is on the main road through the town at the south end – on the right coming from the south after leaving the A9 bypass.

Parking/reception Extensive: enter just south of the distillery. (Disabled parking is about 90yd/80m from reception.) A warm friendly welcome to a modern, architecturally pleasing, visitor centre, which serves as reception, setting-off point and cafeteria. It provides a nice option of a coffee while

waiting to join a tour. Some say the decor is rather kitsch but if so it is carried off with élan.

Tour frequency 20 minutes.

Maximum group size 12

Cost £3.00. Redeemable in shop.

Group bookings By appointment.

Visual aids Excellent audio-visual presentation and good clear diagrams of the step-by-step process.

Foreign visitors Some guides speak foreign languages. Good guide books in shop priced at £3.95.

Photography in distillery? No

Disabled access? Tour restricted by stairs, also in shop area and gallery where the all-important dram is dispensed.

THE PRODUCT

Malt Blair Athol

Owner UDV

Region Highland (southern)

Age 12 years old

Water source Allt Dour – a spring on nearby Ben Vrackie.

Malting At Nairn on the Moray Firth – malt is lightly peated.

Bond A glassed-off viewing area giving a good impression of a traditional warehouse and what goes on in it.

Casks Ex-bourbon

Bottling In Leven and Glasgow.

Experts' opinion Pale amber in colour, full nose with hints of nut and citrus. Medium-sweet body and lingering smoky aftertaste. More a pre-dinner tipple.

Our dram A welcome choice of small or large measures to savour. With 96% of production going to Bell's for blending, Blair Athol is not easy to find but well worth the effort – we bought a bottle in the shop to be on the safe side. A nice amber-gold colour, we found it light with only a hint of peat but a beguiling suggestion of heather.

This is a professional, well thought-out tour, at a comfortable pace covering the stages in distilling clearly and logically. There are touches of humour and a willingness to field questions – even if the answers are not always to hand. On the whole, accurate, informative and fun. There is ample space to move around to see and hear. In a group of 12 we felt part of a family rather than sheep in a flock. Thoroughly enjoyable.

Special features The tour starts with a good introduction to milling with samples of malt and grist. The stainless steel mashtun is followed by no less than eight washbacks. Unusually four are well-proportioned in larch and by contrast four are made of stainless steel. Next come four elegant lacquered copper stills, two wash and two spirit in an attractive setting and then a well-proportioned traditional spirit safe. The cask filling in the spirit store is interesting.

Access Good wide stairs and nice even floors. Access to all the main features of whisky making.

Visual impact Spick and span. A well-laid-out distillery with traditional features. Feels and looks just as you imagine a distillery should.

SHOP

Range A good range of whiskies, decanters, glasses and prints.

Style In an attractive two-storey setting across a courtyard from reception, it is elegant and spacious with a nice air of informality. The tour ends here in the upstairs dram room.

Staff Friendly, helpful and impressively knowledgeable.

Catering Seating for around 40 in an area shared with reception. A good range of scones and cakes with tasty soup and nice fresh sandwiches.

Toilets Those in the reception/cafeteria area are modern and spotless, less so the ones on the first floor of the shop area. Excellent loo in reception for disabled. **Parent and baby** – no facilities but high chair available in café.

SUMMARY

Some distilleries are all too reminiscent of the factories they really are. Blair Athol is different. It looks and feels traditional, with a touch of the essential mystique. It has been accused of being a little twee but if that is so it was probably more evident in the 80s than now. The tour is decidedly on the good side, whether it be your first or one of many, as it offers much. While the shop has a limited range of quality goods, who cares when you have all of Pitlochry's fine shops to squander your money in. A tour is easy to combine with the other holiday attractions of this glorious part of Scotland and is one of the few places you can count on locating a bottle of one of the finer and rarer Southern Highland malts.

Overall rating

DALWHINNIE

Splendid setting and excellent facilities. The tour is basic and hurried.

This is the highest distillery in Scotland at 1073ft/327m above sea level, and has the coldest average recorded temperature in Scotland. Often in winter it is covered in snow, looking bleak and isolated at times but breathtaking when the sun shines. In summer it can be beautiful in the extreme, set in the grandeur of the surrounding hills. The neat and trim distillery buildings, are all that one could wish for, with splendid pagodas, lampposts and those huge, wooden worm tubs. Well worth visiting as it is just as pretty inside as out. There can be snow on the hills even in July.

Established 1898

Enquiries 01540 672219

Website www.scotch.com

Opening hours Easter-Sep, Mon-Sat, 9am-5pm; Sun, 12-5pm; Oct, Mon-Fri, 9am-5pm; Nov-Easter, Mon-Fri, 10am-4pm.

Getting there From A9 heading north from Pitlochry, turn off at first sign for Dalwhinnie. Coming from Inverness, leave A9 six miles/10km before the distillery at the sign for Dalwhinnie. If coming from the west, take the A86 from Spean Bridge and the A889 from Laggan.

Parking/reception Through main entrance on left in front of distillery. Reception is in a splendid building to the left of the car park, combining shop and tour rendezvous point, with flagged granite floors, and a handsome, open-beamed, roof. Its up to you to 'sign-in' for the tour – don't wait to be invited!

Tour frequency Every 20 minutes or so.

Maximum group size 15

Cost £3.50. Redeemable in shop.

Group bookings For visits by larger parties write in advance to Dalwhinnie Distillery, Dalwhinnie, PH19 1AB.

Visual aids Video of malting and model of a still are part of the tour, as is an ancient disused Boby mill.

Foreign visitors Leaflets in Dutch, French, German, Italian, Spanish and Japanese.

Photography in distillery? No

Disabled access? No tour facilities offered – visitor centre only.

THE PRODUCT

Malt   Dalwhinnie

Owner   UDV

Region   Highland (northern)

Ages   15 years old (also double-matured).

Water source Allt an t'Sluie Burn from a spring loch 2000ft (609m) up in the hills.

Malting Carried out at Roseisle, the malted barley is fairly light on phenols. Malting at Dalwhinnie ceased in 1968.

Bond Warehouses on site. As cool as Dalwhinnie – the mean average temperature is 6°c.

Casks Sadly a tantalising glimpse through a small, glass, panel is all the visitor is afforded.

Bottling At Leven in Fife.

Experts' opinion Clean, tight-knit, heather-honey scents 'dancing a brisk reel in the mouth'. Luscious flavour, crisp finish with excellent pre-prandial length to the aftertaste.

Our dram Our sprint tour ended with a modest dram of the regular 15 year old. Age has matured it into a really smooth, sweetish malt, light but with attitude. Definitely a pre-dinner dram but a good 'un.

A fairly basic tour with little 'hands on' to it – no grist to feel or open washbacks to smell. With the size of the groups it can be hard to hear and see. Explanations are pretty stark and bald, and questions are not actively encouraged. The pace is fairly gruelling with little time to savour the handsome stills and other sights. Marshalling is a bit like a race, Did we 'win' doing the whole tour and dram in 15 minutes dead? A hard-sell of Classic Malts range (not perpetrated by other distilleries in the same group) did not help.

Special features The stainless steel mashtun (7-tonne grist capacity), manufactured by Abercrombie of Alloa, sits in the former kiln room under the pagoda chimney. In an attractive bright tun room with imitation oil lamps are six wooden washbacks – the five made of Siberian larch are nearly 50 years old, the youngster is of the more common Oregon pine, but equally handsome. The stillhouse has one wash still and one spirit still, both beautifully lacquered, with worm condensers in huge vats visible on the front wall of the distillery close to the car park. These rare, wooden, worm tubs are reckoned to lead to a slow, deliberate, condensation which can't be matched in conventional condensers and so give Dalwhinnie its extra body. On the other hand it's so blooming cold at Dalwhinnie that the ambient temperature might be the real culprit! The stills are onion-shaped, broad right to the top and have upward-sloping lyne arms – very handsome with nice brass hatches. Abercrombie probably made the elegant spirit safe as well, but it was too far away to be sure. From the tun room there are lovely views of the surrounding countryside.

Access Excellent – wide, open and spacious, but visitors are kept a bit far away from the stills and too far off to see the spirit safe working.

Visual impact Neat, sparkling and cared for. Nice traditional features.

SHOP

Range Dalwhinnie malt, the Classic Malts range and the UDV Rare Malts (at around £60 a bottle) – special bottlings, plus the usual array of glasses and quaichs, books, tapes and some lovely prints.

Style Nicely set out with accessible stands and attractive displays.

Staff Helpful but perhaps too busy to go the extra mile. Have they tasted any of the produce themselves, we wondered?

Catering None – but an interesting art deco hotel is nearby.

Toilets Art deco (something to do with the hotel?), black and white, spick and span. Likewise for disabled. **Parent and baby** – no facilities.

SUMMARY

Once grubby but allegedly endearing, Dalwhinnie Distillery has had the treatment reserved for the Classic Malts distilleries – spruced up, an attractive visitor centre and a quality shop. The experience is compromised by the tour. It's a conveyor belt, frankly. Other distilleries in the same group with larger visitor numbers seem able to cope much better. Difficult to recommend with such a perfunctory and hurried tour. The good news is that with a little effort it could be made better – the setting certainly deserves it.

Overall rating

EDRADOUR

Small is beautiful but has its problems. Too many people and not enough room.

This is really the last of the tiny farm distilleries which were numerous in the 19th century and is composed of an attractive group of whitewashed stone buildings, nestling in a hollow below Ben Vrackie. With the Edradour burn flowing through the site and cottages for all three workers across the way, it makes for an almost film-set sort of beauty. Rowan trees, well-tended grass and the chuckle of the waters flowing by conspire to create an idyllic ambience on a summer's day.

Established 1825

Enquiries 01796 472095

Website www.edradour.com

Opening hours Mar-Oct, Mon-Sat, 9.30am-5pm; Sun, 12-5pm; Nov-Feb, Mon-Sat (shop only), 10am-4pm. Telephone to check first.

Getting there Take the A294 from the centre of Pitlochry, pass through Moulin and a few miles later take a narrow road on the right, signposted Edradour. Road is single-track but not difficult.

Parking/reception Car park is just past the distillery entrance on the right. Walk up beside the Edradour Burn to reception on the right. Unfortunately, chances are there will be no one there to greet you until the next tour is due. There is an interesting display with which to while the time away. Mind your head on entry – this really is the smallest distillery in Scotland! In due course you

will be escorted up to the Malt Barn, where you will savour your free dram before the tour commences.

Tour frequency Every '20 mins for individuals, every half-hour for coaches'.

Maximum group size Too large for comfort – watch out for the coach parties.

Cost Free

Group bookings By appointment

Visual aids Video in the Malt Barn – colourful and visually attractive, but the steps in the process are confusingly out of sequence.

Foreign visitors By prior arrangement for groups, the video can be in French or English with German subtitles.

Photography in distillery? Yes

Disabled access? Malt Barn for video and dram, and when convenient, to the top section of the distillery. The push up the hill with a wheelchair is a daunting prospect.

THE PRODUCT

Malt   The Edradour

Owner   Campbell Distillers

Region   Highland (southern)

Age   10 years old

Water source Springs on Moulin Moor close by.

Malting Guide said malting was done 'locally' but in fact is done in Edinburgh, lightly-peated to Edradour's own specifications.

Bond There is a tiny warehouse on site but most of the whisky is stored in Glasgow.

Casks Ex-oloroso Sherry

Bottling In Glasgow – pictures to view in the reception area.

Experts' opinion Lightly aromatic, slightly dry and malty with an almond taste, and nice balance. A buttery aftertaste and smooth as cream.

Our dram A mite small, but it is free after all! The 'last hand-made malt' is pleasant, smooth with a sweet, smoky tang and constitutes a good introduction to malt.

The tour starts in the Malt Barn, rather bare, large and echoing, but enlivened with the free dram and video. The tour is a bit perfunctory with the steps in the process difficult to follow. Questions are fielded adequately. Despite being told that individual tours were every 20 minutes, groups tend to be large (25+) including the coach parties and in such a small distillery it can be quite difficult to hear, see and ask. Some views are through glass and rather distant – the pace is inevitably slow. Do try not to get engulfed in a Japanese bus party – the tour guides won't save you from that. Bear in mind that a year's production here by only three men is achieved in a week at other distilleries.

Special features A tiny, neat, green and red cast-iron mashtun is the first thing you see. The draff left over which is used as cattle feed does not disappear down a chute here: two thirds of the work-force shovel it out through the window into a waiting cart! After the mashtun comes a nostalgic sight – a cooler which could have come straight from a farm creamery of 50 years ago – a classic Morton. Next two tiny Oregon-pine washbacks and then the rather distant views of the stills – the wash still is a double-onion, and the spirit still straight and dwarf-like, holding a mere 480 gallons (2179 litres).

Access Difficult, simply because it is so small and congested.

Visual impact The novelty comes from the scale – you can take it all in from one spot but you feel remote – 'viewing rather than experiencing' as one fellow visitor said.

SHOP

Range A good choice of whisky and related goods, if rather predictable.

Style Set in a pretty cottage by the burn. Inside the wooden floor gives a rather austere impression.

Staff Friendly and helpful but cut off behind a rather forbidding counter.

Catering No facilities – there is a the hotel in Moulin, and a plethora of restaurants in Pitlochry.

Toilets First-class, attractive, spotlessly clean. Toilet available for the disabled. **Parent and baby** – no facilities.

SUMMARY

Edradour's size is both its biggest attraction and its greatest drawback. Tour groups are too large and the visitor can all too easily become engulfed in a huge group. Most things are done well within the physical limitations, but you will see and experience at first-hand much more elsewhere. Despite the constraints, the ambience and the sheer dinkiness draw a host of visitors each year – many of whom return again.

Overall rating

FETTERCAIRN

No frills friendly tour and the best video on distilling. Watch out for the 'self-cooling' stills.

The town of Fettercairn, entered through a stone arch commemorating a visit by Queen Victoria, lies in the Mearns, a fertile carse bounded by the foothills of the Grampians. The distillery stands out, white and proud in the fields where rich barley harvests led to its establishment in 1824 in a former corn mill. White and neat, it seems just right for the job – no fancy gardens or picnic areas, but in keeping with the place and its people. Inside it is suitably old in feel, ideal for its purpose, and an excellent example of a good traditional distillery. Perhaps Victoria was visiting Gladstone when she graced Fettercairn with her presence – the family seat at Gasque is just up the road – house, grounds and deer park are open to the public, May to September, and are well worth visiting.

Established 1824

Enquiries 01561 340205

Website None

Opening hours May-Sep, Mon-Sat, 10am-4.30pm.

Getting there From the A90 take the B966 to Fettercairn and follow the signs. From Deeside take the scenic B974 over the Cairn o' Mount.

Parking/reception Car park is just after the distillery entrance, on the right: it has high walls – take care when leaving. Follow the signs to reception from the car park – about a hundred yards or so and up some steps (guides will show you an alternative way for wheelchairs). On arrival you will get a really warm welcome, conveyed in a lovely Mearns accent. Staff will emerge from behind a counter complete with spirit safe and an old style teller's window, take you next-door to the theatre for a dram and a 10-minute video. You sit in wooden chairs for all the world like those in a Scots kirk.

Tour frequency As required.

Maximum group size 25 but smaller numbers are preferred.

Cost Free.

Group bookings By appointment with reception.

Visual aids Tour starts with probably the best video around. Locally made, it is rich in colour, has just enough carefully selected history, and an admirably lucid description of distilling, using shots taken with affection at Fettercairn by local film makers.

Foreign visitors Leaflets in several languages including Japanese.

Photography in distillery? No

Disabled access? Reasonable, but the distance between some features can be a little daunting.

THE PRODUCT

Malt	Old Fettercairn
Owner	JBB (Greater Europe) plc
Region	Highland (eastern)
Ages	10, 26 & 30 years old

Water source An unnamed spring two miles (3.2km) away in the Cairngorms, piped in for distillation.

Malting Carried out by maltsters at Arbroath or further north at Montrose or Buckie. It is lightly peated.

Bond There are 15 bonded warehouses on site – traditional racks three barrels high and earthen floors. There is a viewing gallery and cooperage display.

Casks Ex-bourbon, sherry and refill whisky.

Bottling Leith, near Edinburgh

Experts' opinion Light, dryish nose with hints of malt and vanilla. Medium weight, slightly dry, spicy and creamy. A good all-rounder.

Our dram A quality malt often available at a reasonable price, our dram did not disappoint (even at 10am) – straw-gold in colour, with a malty, smoky taste and a wee hint of sweetness.

A fair bit of walking – much of it outside – is involved, but it is a good complement to the video and everything falls nicely into place. Guides are knowledgeable and committed. They handle questions competently with a quiet touch or two of humour. Plenty of room to see and hear, and at a pace which gives you time – not one of these places where the guide seems to have a deadline to meet!

Special features An unusually graceful mashtun forged in cast iron with a suitably elegant copper cover and a capacity of five tonnes of grist. An old-fashioned horizontal agitator runs on cogs around the inside rim. The old, redundant, wort cooler (resplendent in brass and featured in the video) can be spotted, but not its replacement. Eight conventional Oregon-pine washbacks bubble away – interestingly the yeast is added in dry form at Fettercairn. Also unique to Fettercairn are the external water-cooling jackets of the upper sections of the wash stills where any traces of yeast still present can lead to the wash boiling over the top if the staff are less than alert. For another variation on this visit Dalmore, owned by the same group. There are two pairs of stills, side-by-side, and of similar size – tubby with stocky tops, straight, broad swan necks and pretty copper condensers. One still was made by Blair of Glasgow, another by Grant of Dufftown: the other two seem to have been by 'anon'. The two spirit safes are difficult to see in detail when the stills are working. MacMillan of Prestonpans manufactured them, so at least three famous names in the distilling supply trades have been at work in Fettercairn.

Access Overall this is good – would be less fun on a rainy day. When the distillery is working you can't get close enough to the stills and spirit safe.

Visual impact Intimate, neat, cared for, largely traditional. Main features in one main well-lit hall.

SHOP

Range The malts made by the owning group (Jim Bean Brands), china eagles and owls, jams and pickles (own brand) and lovely water-colour prints of Fettercairn – we bought one!

Style Like an old-fashioned shop with a real counter and period lighting.

Staff Shop manned by the guides who are a delight to meet – patient and cheery.

Catering None

Toilets Clean, white, bright and pine – small but who needs to swing a cat in the loo? Likewise for disabled. **Parent and baby** – no facilities

SUMMARY

There is no finer run for scenery than from Angus over Cairn o' Mount to Deeside and a visit to Fettercairn will enhance that sublime experience. There are no frills, but the folk are friendly, the video is the tops, the tour a good one and the mashtun and the self-cooling stills worth seeing in their own right. Equally fascinating for the first-timer and the veteran alike.

Overall rating

GLENTURRET

A little gem – one of the most popular. Perpetually pristine and sparkling. Ace tour, top visitor centre and the Smugglers Restaurant excels in Scottish fare.

Described in 1887 as 'one of the prettiest Glens of all Scotland'. Glenturret is in a beautiful spot: surrounded by lush tree-clad hills with the Turret burn meandering by. A little wooden bridge leads across the burn to a tranquil walk in the glen. Despite being small and busy, Glenturret is immaculate inside and out – trim, white farm buildings and a magnificent modern visitor centre exquisitely sculptured on a little rise alongside. There are picnic tables by the burn, verandas to sun yourself on and an almost continental feel about the place, bustling but relaxed. Somehow even a 120ft/36m-high chimney doesn't seem to be out of place. Commercial yes, but a major tourist attraction which avoids the pitfalls of vulgarity.

Established 1775

Enquiries 01764 656565

Website www.glenturret.com

Opening hours Mar-Dec, Mon-Sat, 9.30am-6pm; Sun, 12-6pm; Jan, Mon-Fri, 11.30am-4pm; Feb, Mon-Sat, 11.30am-4pm, free entry during 'silent season'. Jan-Feb, last tour 2.30pm.

Getting there Take the A85 Oban road from Crieff, turn right on the outskirts at the signpost for Glenturret Distillery. If coming from the north then leave the A822 at the signpost for Monzie.

Parking/reception There is ample parking just past the distillery on the right. Reception is a spacious and airy hall with reception desk and touchscreen videos to help you find your bearings. A cheery welcome awaits.

Tour frequency Every 20 minutes.

Maximum group size 25

Cost £3.50 with one tasting sample (£3.00 for senior citizens). Family, £9.00, 12-17 year olds, £2.30. Under-12s are free.

Group bookings For 40 or more.

Visual aids Touchscreen facilities at reception. After the tour and the dram a 10-minute video – lively pictures but a little too long perhaps. This is followed by the 'Spirit of the Glen' exhibition with three-dimensional scenes which are excellent on malting and cooperage in particular.

Foreign visitors Information sheets available at reception in French, German, Swedish, Dutch, Spanish and Italian.

Photography in distillery? No

Disabled access? Possible to reach everything on the tour as well as the Smugglers Restaurant via a ramp behind.

THE PRODUCT

Malt	The Glenturret
Owner	Highland Distillers
Region	Highland (southern)
Ages	12, 15, 18, 21, (25 & 27 sold out for now!) and a liqueur.

Water source Loch Turret a few miles away, feeding a tank just across the road from the distillery.

Malting 'Prisma' Barley supplied by Simpsons of Berwick, only lightly peated.

Bond Viewing of the casking room and the smallest of six on-site bonded warehouses.

Casks Ex-sherry, bourbon and refill whisky.

Bottling In Glasgow. Nearly all (80%) of it comes back to be sold in the shop!

Experts' opinion Honey, soft, smooth with peat and vanilla. One of the finest Highland malts, a good depth of flavour and admirable consistency.

Our dram In the tasting room at the visitor centre – pale, with a nice sweet nose. Smooth taste, almost a Lowland feel to it. Not a lot of peat but a lot of 'character'.

A first-class tour of a small but pretty distillery – the oldest working one in Scotland. Everything you should see on a tour is included, in an orderly way. It lasts 25 minutes plus the film and exhibition. Friendly guides field questions more than competently – ours was an expert on distillery plumbing!

Special features Good pace and clear views. This is the most visited distillery in Scotland but groups are skilfully kept apart – seemingly without effort. You start at the Porteous mill, working away with wooden elevators and other pieces of plant, then on to the mashtun, which is positively tiny – only 5ft/1.5m deep, lidless and with railings – unusual, pretty, and with an discarded perforated base set in the floor adjacent, making it easy to visualise how it worked. The tunroom, for all the world like an old farm byre, contains eight Oregon-pine, pocket-sized washbacks – 'guid gear in sma' bulk'. The stills, one wash and one smaller spirit still, are biggish, with their necks seeming almost to soar straight through the pitched roof. The wash still has a curvaceous onion, a splendid brass band around its waist and straight sides. The spirit still, half-a-floor down (gravity works!) is plain and workmanlike. Make sure the guide allows you outside and round to see it at close quarters; while out there you can view the copper condensers. A nicely proportioned spirit safe sits atop splendid copper pipes feeding the wooden-topped spirit receiver. The casking room with its 'petrol pump' cask filler and weighing machine is interesting too, as is the range of cask sizes. The dinky tun, tubs and stills are a delight – you feel you want to take them home with you!

Access Excellent – very few stairs – there are only a few on the way up to the tun room.

Visual impact Intimate, very reminiscent of its farm origins: unspoiled. The description, 'like the buildings, the vessels are of the ancient pattern', is as true today as it was when written by a visitor 120 years ago.

Range You name it, they have it – teeshirts, woollens, skirts in Glenturret tartan as well as hats, scarves, glasses, crystal decanters, CDs, confectionery, jugs n' mugs, hampers, foods, books (even one for the kids on Towser, the distillery cat who lived for 24 years and killed 28,899 mice! And finally Glenturret malt!

Style Vast, commercial outlet, bright airy and business-like – a triumph of marketing.

Staff Hard-pressed with queues at coach party time, but friendly enough.

Catering This could be the best in the distillery business. The Smugglers Restaurant is self-service (posh folks or conference-goers can try the Pagoda Room with waitresses) and there is an open-air veranda complete with sun umbrellas. Meals are served 12 noon to 3pm; soup and sandwiches till 5pm, and coffee till 6pm. Prices are reasonable, with a childrens' menu as well. Soup, sandwiches (£2.50), salads and hot dishes are all of excellent quality – try the haddock in whisky batter – yum! – a bargain at £5.50. Or the haggis, neeps and tatties at £4.95. This is Scottish fare at its very best.

Toilets Well-appointed, spotless, plush and adjacent to the Smugglers Restaurant. Excellent loos at reception for disabled. **Parent and baby** – adjacent to dining area in the visitor centre.

One of Scotland's top tourist attractions with quarter of a million pilgrims a year from around the world. The distillery is so small that by rights it should look worn, well-used and down-at-heel. Not a bit of it – it sparkles. It is a matter of perpetual wonder how such a pretty little gem, with excellent tours, can co-exist with and be complemented by a state-of-the-art visitor centre offering the best of Scottish fare to eat, drink and carry off in plastic bags. The complete experience without question. Or rather with one final question ... who was counting the mice!

Overall rating

ROYAL LOCHNAGAR

Repackaged to be less touristy. Much for the educated visitor but low on the fun factor.

You can't do better than Deeside, especially with the Windsors as next-door neighbours. Set in a bowl of pines with the Low Dam beside it, the distillery is an impressive sight – grey granite which glistens come rain or shine. The pagoda rises imperiously above the line of reception and distillery buildings. Nonetheless there is an austere air about it all – signalling that one should be in a suitably serious frame of mind. This is going to be heavier on the education than the frivolity.

Established 1845

Enquiries 01339 742700

Website None

Opening hours Easter-Sep, Mon-Sat, 10am-5pm; Sun, 12-4pm; Oct-Easter, Mon-Fri, 10am-4pm. Under-8s are welcome but not encouraged to take the tour.

Getting there From the main A93 Deeside road, take the B976 signposted for Balmoral. After a while you will spot the distillery sign on the right.

Parking/reception The first thing you see as you approach is a long, low, building fronting the distillery. The combined shop and reception area has bare floors and walls which lack warmth, as does the reception – polite, but a touch perfunctory. After paying, there is a chance to explore a small exhibition area, press buttons on a video which is heavy on royal connections, and relax in a pleasant conservatory-style waiting room.

Tour frequency Every 15-20 mins.

Maximum group size 15

Cost £4.00. Redeemable in shop.

Group bookings Bus parties are discouraged. Other groups should book ahead.

Visual aids Video in waiting area. Small non-involving exhibition.

Foreign visitors Information sheets available in six languages but guides say they do not cater for non-English speaking visitors!

Photography in distillery? No

Disabled access? Disabled visitors are given a good ground-floor tour and can see most of what is available.

THE PRODUCT

Malt   Royal Lochnagar

Owner   UDV

Region   Highland (eastern)

Ages 12 years and Selected Reserve, the special bottling on the 12th Sept each year to commemorate the anniversary of Queen Victoria's visit. At close to £200 a bottle, it's good with some quite old malts in it, but it's not that good! We'd have six bottles of Longrow or five of Macallan instead!

Water source From the top dam (it has a peat base) which draws from the burn running through the ground. The bottom dam alongside the distillery is used for cooling.

Malting At Roseisle, Elgin.

Bond Some at the distillery and the rest at Alloa in Central Scotland. Visitors enjoy a good view of the warehouse from the erstwhile kiln room.

Casks Ex-sherry and bourbon. Royal Lochnager uses a higher proportion than is usual of refill whisky casks – which gives the characteristic lighter colour and taste.

Bottling At Leven in Fife.

Experts' opinion Pale with gold highlights, and a sweet, fruity nose. Good body, creamy, nut-sweet, with a smooth accomplished finish.

Our dram Administered in the kiln room – smooth, creamy, full-bodied with a distinctive individualistic nose – a clean, sherry, ever-so-slightly smoky aftertaste – very moreish.

TOUR EXPERIENCE

This tour is aimed at the serious visitor and succeeds in that very well. It is of high quality, with guides clearly able to tailor the level to suit the particular needs of the individual visitor. Depth of knowledge is impressive. Leisurely pace – 45 minutes or so, allows time to see, absorb and query. More of an itinerant conversation than a school crocodile.

Special features A smallish, red, Boby mill with fresh and malted barley samples, together with grist (properly explained as 20% husk, 70% 'grits' and 10% flour) then on to a most unusual open-topped and capacious mashtun; modern-looking but curiously with the old-fashioned horizontal agitator, manufactured by Abercrombie of Alloa. Staff reckon the steam from the mashing process dissipates simply through good ventilation. The absence of a cover certainly makes for an excellent view. Surrounding copper pipes are reminiscent of the *Lusitania* (not the *Titanic*!). Looking through a glass-fronted honeycomb cooler is fun as the wort trickles through. The three washbacks are made of Scottish larch with a life expectancy of up to 40 years. You are allowed to view the process through glass partitions. In the stillroom, which has a nice varnished roof, are two well-cared-for stubby stills – a bit like inverted wine glasses. The wash still is the larger of the two: both have broad, straight swan necks and are not so tall as to promote much reflux. Abercrombie provided the external worm condensers (which sadly you cannot see) – unusual to say the least. The spirit safe sits atop a brown, cast-iron, low wines receiver close to a handsome, dark, oak spirit receiver. The kiln remains much as it was and it is easy to imagine how the peat smoke once filled this space and dried the germinating barley. The one warehouse on site is untypically three storeys high.

Access Generally good and relatively easy, except to the tun room, where the view through a glass partition inevitably cuts you off from the smell and froth of fermentation – access is possible if you specifically request it. We suggest you do.

Visual impact Immaculate, a good spectacle. The copper pipeworks and the stills are polished every Friday and it shows. They are fab!

SHOP

Range Apart from a reasonable selection of books, it concentrates exclusively on malts – the Classic Malts range, Royal Lochnagar and about 70 others. It is good but being confined largely to UDV group products, is not quite as comprehensive as one might expect.

Style Back-lit display cases, and a long counter – a little remote and clinical.

Staff Friendly but reticent about offering help. If you ask, they will willingly let you nose the Classic Malts, but the inevitable question arises – have they actually tasted much of the range themselves?

Catering None. The coffee shop which was once here is sadly missed. Training facilities for UDV group staff are no substitute. Simply put ... the public are not catered for.

Toilets Adequate but would benefit from a bit of 'tlc' so evident in the distillery itself. Good toilet facilities for the disabled. Clean and well cared for. **Parent and baby** – combined with the disabled toilet. A good facility.

SUMMARY

Recently Royal Lochnagar has been re-packaged to be less touristy and more specialist. The distillery brochure surprisingly extols the range of malts in the shop rather than the distillery visit itself. Perhaps they haven't got it all worked out yet, but while the tour is excellent, and guides can easily cope with those visitors who wish to parade their erudition, somehow it is less relaxed than other smaller distilleries. Perhaps Lochnagar is a bit overshadowed by its Classic Malts sister distilleries? But it is well worth visiting, have no doubt, and the 12 year old is seriously potable. A wee bit low on the fun factor and in need of a bit of buzz.

Overall rating

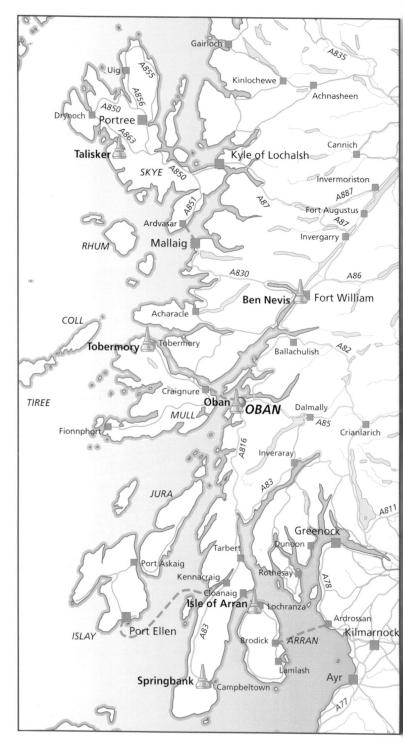

The Islands & The West Coast

TOURING CENTRE: OBAN

This is a huge area which possesses the unique qualities of the islands and the 'almost island' of the Mull of Kintyre. Islay and Jura logically belong to this area, but having so many distilleries must merit their own section (see pages 44-59). Oban has been chosen as the main centre because it is possible (just) to visit any one of the six distilleries in a day from there. A visit to Skye should involve an overnight stay and we like The Tables Hotel in Dunvegan (01470 521404) which just about accepts bikers, or the primitive but splendid campsite at Sligachan. For an overnight stay in Campbeltown, the Ardsheil Hotel (01586 552133) is recommended for dinner, bed and breakfast. Arran boasts many fine boarding houses of which our pick is the Black Rock in Corrie (01770 810282). Combine this with dinner at the Isle of Arran Distillery. A really pleasant caravan site exists at the Lochranza golf course (01770 830600).

Oban has the finest situation of any town of its size in the United Kingdom, and is the gateway to the islands, via the ubiquitous Caledonian MacBrayne ferries. Combine a visit to Tobermory Distillery with one to the sacred Isle of Iona and try out the glorious, twisty short cut from Salen to the A984. And don't miss out on a dinner cruise from Oban to Colonsay or Coll and Tiree. If you must have bagpipes, kilts and kitsch, try the nightly ceilidhs at Mactavish's Kitchen near the distillery.

Our recommendations for bed, views and cordon bleu cooking would be Ards House at Connel (01631 710255) and for the freshest of seafood, the Pierhouse at Port Appin (01631 730302) – but insist on a window table. The best caravan site in Scotland, bar none, is run by the delightful Peter and Katie Weir (in association with the Caravan Club) at North Ledaig just beyond Connel on the A828.

For bikers we recommend the 18th-century inn at Lagg, Kilmory on Arran (01770 870255) which is a convenient spot for lunch on a ride round the island from the piers at Brodick and Lochranza. Kilchurn at Connel (01631 710581) understands the needs of bikers well. For everyone, fish and chips from the Happy Chippie on the main street in Oban is best savoured on the seafront while admiring the passing yachts and ferries. If you fancy something a bit posher the Bistro at the Falls of Lora Hotel (01631 710483) is pretty reliable and reasonably priced.

BEN NEVIS

ISLE OF ARRAN

OBAN

SPRINGBANK

TALISKER

TOBERMORY

Aimed at the bus party and for something to do on a wet day. Kids will like Hamish McDram

In the shadow of Ben Nevis, the distillery looks like a neat creamery with a brick chimney and grey slate roof – there is nothing of the traditional distillery silhouette. It would have suited an ancient islander of our acquaintance who took half-a-pint of milk in his dram! Staff set out to attract visitors looking for a holiday experience rather than those who thirst for knowledge but that fits in well with an atmosphere which is down-market yet honest with few concessions to glamour. Everything is clean but nothing is sparkling. The upside is that there is nothing intimidating and there is a friendly feel. However, it is hard work to get a clear picture of all the parts of the process from malting to the finished spirit maturing in the cask. The manager confided in us that would-be aficionados should try Tuesday mornings when production staff can be found conducting the tours.

Established 1825

Enquiries 01397 700200

Website www.bennevis.co.uk

Opening hours All year, Mon-Fri, 9am-5pm; Jul-Aug, Mon-Fri, 9am-7.30pm; late Jun-Sep, Sat, 10am-4pm.

Getting there On A82 – two miles (3.2km) north of Fort William on the right opposite BP filling station just past the Mallaig junction heading towards Inverness.

Parking/reception At front of distillery – wide entrance. Swing round to the right. Friendly enough reception area but a little gloomy and pokey. Display boards dauntingly wordy – information overload could provide a PhD thesis on the history of the founder!

Tour frequency Half-hourly when busy, hourly on the hour at other times.

Maximum group size '15', (we had 27!)

Cost £2.00. Redeemable in shop.

Group bookings By appointment.

Visual aids A good film with some humour on the history of the distillery recounted by Hamish MacDram. Nothing on the process. Amusing for the kids.

Foreign visitors On request, leaflets in Japanese, French, German, Italian, Spanish and Gaelic.

Photography in distillery? Yes

Disabled access Good to the visitor centre, poor to the distillery. Possible to view the stills from the ground floor only.

THE PRODUCT

Malt	Ben Nevis
Owner	Ben Nevis Distillery (Fort William) Ltd
Region	Highland (western)
Ages	8, 10 & 26 years old

Water source Coire Leis and Coire Na Ciste, drawing water off the Alllt a Mhullin Burn at a point about 750ft/228m above sea level.

Malting Malted barley is brought in from Tain in Sutherland and is fairly heavily peated.

Bond No access for visitors.

Casks Ex-sherry, French wine and bourbon. Our guide pointed out three sizes of cask.

Bottling Carried out at Invergordon, north of Inverness.

Experts' opinion 26 year old at around £75 a bottle is medium-dry, full-bodied smooth with a smoky, long-lasting aftertaste.

Our dram What a surprise – the tour ends with a Ben Nevis blend of no great distinction. If you fancy a 10-year-old malt it will set you back another £1.50. We refrained. The guide says that the blend has won an award and that most folk prefer blends anyway. They deny that it is a money-saving measure! We felt a little hard done by and were far from alone in that.

TOUR EXPERIENCE

This was distinctly average – difficult to follow, lacking in depth, although the guide is friendly and ready to answer questions, if at times inaudible which tends to make some, especially children, lose interest. The guide told us later that talking quietly made folk concentrate but sadly, on this occasion at least, the evidence was against him. We went round in a group of 27 which was simply far too many, especially as there were no aids or diagrams to help. The route, however, was well thought out, which was just as well with so many folk milling about.

Special features Mashtun and washbacks are of stainless steel, albeit with nice tooling on the covers and have a utilitarian appearance – for realists rather than romantics. The stills are more memorable for their plumbing than their aesthetics but have a certain robust charm, working in pairs on a raised platform where visitors can peer in when they are not in use. The four copper stills, two wash and two spirit, could do with a bit of polishing but their age and size impress. Two are original patterns from 1825, and the other two date from 1865 although they have only been in situ since 1955.

Access There are rather a lot of stairs and passageways through a fairly modern building which makes for a rather gruelling experience. Watch out for a large bell just as you set off which might make your head ring, and puddles on the floors. Not an ideal place for the less than spry.

Visual impact You soon get the message that this is a working factory with few concessions to the mystique of the whisky-making process.

SHOP

Range Better to make for Fort William and browse the Scotch Whisky Shop, MacLennan's Whisky Centre and The Scottish Crafts and Whisky Centre – all in the Main Street.

Style All glass cases and displays – nothing to get your hands on.

Staff Helpful and friendly.

Catering Sharing space with the shop is a cosy tearoom with a good range of yummy home-made scones, cakes and shortbread at very reasonable prices. Between noon and 2pm you can sample a baked potato, fresh sandwiches or hot soup – we strongly recommend the tomato and carrot. Tea, coffee and soft drinks are available. We met a chap who always arranges to lunch here when in the area.

Toilets Adequate but bring your own loo paper! No disabled toilet. **Parent and baby** – no facilities.

SUMMARY

There are more beautiful distilleries with greater aesthetic appeal and better-stocked shops in which to be parted from one's money. There are undoubtedly better tours with more to see, and yet there is something to be said for the friendly honesty of Ben Nevis. If you want a taste of the whisky experience without too much commitment of time and effort, this could be for you and for the youngsters, who will enjoy the company of Hamish MacDram. On a dreich West Highland day, a cuppa and a scone in the cosy tearoom could round off a pleasant, if unexciting experience.

Overall rating

ISLE OF ARRAN

New, compact and pretty. Good tour and award-winning restaurant.

Arran is a magic island ('Scotland in miniature') and Lochranza ('ransa' is from the Norse for the rowan trees which abound) has everything – castle ruins, burns, pier, bay and hills. The distillery buildings are all similar in shape and are small enough to match the scale of the local architecture. They echo the kilns and pagodas of older distilleries, and do so to good purpose. The views from the distillery and restaurant are stunning – even from the car park, they take some beating. This is a modern tourist attraction with no more than a hint of kitsch, and with something for everyone.

Established 1995

Enquiries 01770 830334

Website www.arranwhisky.com

Opening hours Apr-Oct, every day, 10am-6pm. Winter opening times vary – see local press.

Getting there Take the Arran ferry from Ardrossan (in Ayrshire) to Brodick or from Claonaig (in Kintyre) to Lochranza. The distillery is on the main A841 just north of Lochranza. Enter into a rough-surfaced car park. Disabled visitors should enter by a smoother entrance on the Lochranza side.

Parking/reception Reception is signposted a little to the right of the car park and is modern and welcoming. A central hall contains an exhibition complete with waving barley in a highland setting. Plenty to read and browse as you await the start of your tour – alternatively pop upstairs for a coffee and home-baked scone.

Tour frequency On the hour from 10am.

Maximum group size 18

Cost £3.50 for adults and £2.50 for students. Redeemable in shop. Under-12s are free.

Group bookings For group bookings contact Tom Pearson.

Visual aids A seven-minute video is part of the tour – colourful but uninformative with a bit too much 'sell'. Everything on the tour is clearly labelled.

Foreign visitors Good leaflets in Dutch, French, German, Italian, Japanese, Portuguese, Spanish and Swedish.

Photography in distillery? Yes

Disabled access There is a lift to the restaurant. Stairs are an obstacle to the distillery 'hall', but mid-week there are always willing hands to help.

THE PRODUCT

Malt Isle of Arran

Owner Isle of Arran Distillers Ltd

Region Islands

Age Six years and maturing nicely.

Water source Loch na Davie a few miles away from which it flows over red granite.

Malting Malted at Pencaitland in Lothian. Lightly peated and, most unusually, delivered as grist.

Bond Two attractive warehouses on site with another projected. Meanwhile some casks slumber at Springbank's warehouses in Campbeltown.

Casks Ex-bourbon and sherry

Bottling At Invergordon

Experts' opinion White corn colour, youthful aroma, fruity with a clean barley maltiness – a hint of sea breeze. Slight oily in texture – appetizing finish – a promising dram which will only get better.

Our dram We had a choice of five-year-old malt, Lochranza blend, or Holy Isle Cream Liqueur (with Irish cream!). We tasted the malt – exceptional for a malt so young. This augurs well for the future – a peppery temptresss – soft, malty with a long finish. Seems to be twice its age (a compliment to a malt, if not to a lady!).

An excellent tour in a distillery recently built with visitors specifically in mind – everything is in one hall with oodles of space and excellent lighting. Tour content is accurate, informative, laced with humour and there is always a ready response to questions. Suitable for both tyros and veteran visitors. Almost no marshalling is needed. Pity you miss out on milling – so sadly there is no grist to smell and feel. You also miss out on a warehouse visit.

Special features The tour starts with introductions and then a video watched in an 18th-century 'Cottage' with grate and flagged floors. This feature is not keyed in enough to the rest of the tour and you wonder a bit why you are there. Then on to the distillery which is on one floor in a hall with twin pagoda-style, wooden, beamed roofs echoing those of traditional kilns. There are exquisite glimpses of the hills by courtesy of the skylights. Everything is small scale – a tiny stainless steel mashtun with a superb copper lid and water pipes, then four washbacks, equally compact at only 15,000 litres (3300 gallons) capacity. Three were built originally in Oregon pine and a fourth was built on site by coopers in five days – and not a single leak! This one is in Norwegian spruce and is slightly lighter in colour. The stills were made by Forsyth of Rothes (one of only two still makers still in business). The coppersmiths produced a wash still (7,100 litres/1563 gallons) and a spirit still (4,300 litres/947 gallons) which are relatively tall and slender with an almost horizontal lyne arm and elegant condensers – all pristine and highly lacquered. The brass spirit safe is unremarkable but satisfyingly in proportion. Both spirit receivers are oak 'barrels' and have quaint safety rails on top – clearly a triumph for a Health and Safety bureaucrat from the mainland!

Access Could not be easier – one flight of stairs and all is revealed.

Visual impact Neat, compact – a modern setting for traditional distilling – pretty stills and washbacks.

Range Isle of Arran malts and blends, glasses, flasks, candles, books, cufflinks, – wood craft, fleeces, shirts and caps, umbrellas, haggis, mustard – and a range of preserves, pickles and other edibles.

Style Cream walls, recessed lights, blue carpet – a feeling of purse-opening euphoria is induced.

Staff Tour Manager Bob and his staff will cater for every whim and then some!

Catering Harold's Restaurant, open 10am to 5pm for tea, coffee and delicious home baking. Lunch 12.30-2.30. Dinner 7pm-9pm except Mondays (award-winning Scottish fare). Tour visitors should not miss lunch – starters include smoked salmon and Cullen Skink (the best fish soup bar none) and can be followed by anything from a fresh filled baguette to mussels, salmon or an excellent pasta. The views from the balcony setting, with windows in the roof, complement the wonderful food, and friendly attentive service.

Toilets Modern, plentiful and excellent in every way. Disabled loos on both levels. **Parent and baby** – nappy-changing in downstairs disabled toilet. High chairs available in Harold's Restaurant.

The rebirth of distilling in Arran was as exciting as it was unexpected. The distillery tour is a pretty good experience compared to that at a traditional distillery – perhaps better in its contemporary compactness. The setting is splendid and the catering is first-class, morning, afternoon and evening. The staff are enthusiastic and friendly. To complete the picture, and to the great relief of all involved, the malt bids fair to becoming a classic in due course.

Overall rating

OBAN

In the top echelon of tours. Classic distillery in urban setting. Quality facilities and visual aids.

The distillery lies on a cramped site in the middle of Oban overlooking the bay with glorious views of Kerrera and distant Mull and with a sheer rock face immediately behind. Lift your eyes even higher and you can admire McCaig's Tower (call it a folly at your peril!). Urban, cluttered, and half-obscured by some unfortunate out-of-period shop fronts in George Street, there are still signs of former grandeur – sadly the pagoda kilns have not survived. Happily it is much more pleasant inside than out and handy for the shops and piers.

Established 1794

Enquiries 01631 572004

Website www.scotch.com

Opening hours All year, Mon-Fri, 9.30am-5pm; Easter-Oct, Sat, 9.30am-5pm; Jul-Sep, Mon-Fri, 9.30am-8.30pm; Jul-Sep, Sun 12-5pm. Dec-Feb, restricted tours – by appointment only.

Getting there In Stafford Street, Oban, opposite the bay, close to the North Pier. Reach Oban by the A85 from Crianlarich or the A816 from Lochgilphead.

Parking/reception No parking at the distillery. There is park-and-ride to left of the A85 on the hill down to the town, and parking behind the station and on the pier close to the distillery. Oban can be congested in summer. First impressions are of a spartan, warehousey feel – correct rather than warm. Reception is restrained and business-like, as one is ushered upstairs to the Tour Collection room (the former malting floor) which contains an excellent visual history of Oban and the distillery's founding family. There is a beautifully compiled, but slightly out-of-focus, DIY video to while away the waiting time.

Tour frequency Half-hourly or less if busy.

Maximum group size 15

Cost £3.50. Redeemable in shop.

Group bookings By appointment with reception staff.

Visual aids High quality charts trace the distilling process. There are really good and informative videos on malting and on cooperage – aspects often neglected on tours.

Foreign visitors Informative boards at each stopping point in French, German and Spanish.

Photography in distillery? No

Disabled access Lift to the Tour Collection room. Distillery tour not feasible.

THE PRODUCT

Malt Oban

Owner UDV

Region Highland (western)

Age 14 years old

Water source Two lochs in Ardconnel, a mile (1.6km) behind the distillery.

Malting Shown on the video – now carried out in the Nairn area, with lightly-peated flavour imparted to the malted barley.

Bond A section is cut out of the wall to permit visitors to peer in and assimilate the feeling of timelessness as the whisky matures. You will have to imagine the aromas.

Casks Ex-bourbon

Bottling Bottling now takes place at Leven in Fife. The tour includes the former filling store which, with the cooperage display and video, gives a good clear picture.

Experts' opinion Merits its place among UDV's Classic Malts range with a delicate, creamy, sweetness. Smooth, peppery with a hint of heather.

Our dram The tour ends with a generous dram of Oban malt and a soft-sell of the six Classic Malts range. Oban is delectable with a hint of peat but mellow and malty. It is neither Highland nor Island but a bit of both ... the best bits.

This is in the top echelon of tours. The route is well-planned and logical with stops where everyone can see and hear the first-class explanations given by the guides. The latter are friendly with clearly spontaneous improvisation, and infectious humour. They handle questions with an easy competence. There is plenty of space and firm, but pleasant, control and congenial pace ensure that there is no excuse for failing to take it all in.

Special features A nice compact feel about things. The mashtun looks rather clinical in stainless steel, but the four Oregon-pine washbacks more than compensate – stainless steel is reputedly easier to clean, but wood is warmer and more user-friendly. The stills – one wash still and one spirit, are relatively small but have a tall, narrow, elegance with narrowish lyne arms. The stillroom is a bit cramped, as is the whole site, which may explain why there are still only the original two stills despite frequent expansion plans. The spirit safe is all that one could hope for – polished brass, elegant and easy to understand.

Access Good, convenient and well-planned: stairs are safe and well-lit. There is space to see everything.

Visual impact Despite its town location, Oban has a real distillery feel – handsome washbacks and stills grab the eye.

Range Limited to the six Classic Malts and the branded glasses from which to quaff them.

Style A wee mite stark and utilitarian – more Kwik-Save than Sainsbury!

Staff Couldn't be more approachable, knowledgeable and helpful. The latent warmth shows through here.

Catering None, but literally a stone's throw away is MacTavish's Kitchen: just the place for haggis, neeps and tatties, or simply a drop scone and a cappuccino. Kitsch ceilidhs happen here on summer evenings.

Toilets Modern, clean and well-looked after. Toilet for disabled available. **Parent and baby** – no facilities.

A visit here is a first-class experience guaranteed to enrich any holiday in Argyll and the Isles, especially on one of those rare days when Kerrera is obscured by a Scotch mist or Lorne is in the monsoon season. The tour is as good as any: clear, informative, and downright enjoyable. High marks for the visual displays, the humour, and the delectable dram. NOTE: It is wise to book in advance from June through to September.

Overall rating

SPRINGBANK

A hidden jewel: fiercely independent with everything from malting to bottling on site. Top-rate tour with all the traditional sights and aromas from peat to spirit – just grand!

Stuck in the middle of Campbeltown, surrounded by buildings, there is nothing remarkable about the site. There are no pagodas (real or designer) to see, but the buildings have an honest, whitewashed, antiquity abounding in wheels and pulleys, which is quite arresting in its own way. Campbeltown, with its loch and seafront is well worth the journey down the beautiful Mull of Kintyre, either by the main A83 or the spectacular single-track B842 via Carradale, which goes on to Southend where Ireland is plainly visible on a clear day.

Established 1828

Enquiries 01586 552085

Website None

Opening hours Apr-Oct, Mon-Thu, 2pm-3.15pm.

Getting there Take the A83 down the Mull of Kintyre to Campbeltown. The distillery is in Long Row which is the main road to the town centre and it lies on the right behind the Springbank Evangelical Church. Material for a sermon on the evils of alcohol?

Parking/reception Enter by the sign on the wall and up a narrow lane: park on the left opposite the distillery gates. Facing you as you enter the gate is the office in a small cottage with roses round the door. Pay the lady in the office (having booked first), and collect the ticket for your miniature. Sit on a barrel in the sun (perpetual in Kintyre) and await the arrival of your guide at 2pm, then off you go.

Tour frequency At 2.00pm.

Maximum group size 15

Cost £3.00 (children free).

Group bookings By appointment only.

Visual aids None

Foreign visitors No facilities – but guide has good clear pronunciation.

Photography in distillery? Yes

Disabled access None

THE PRODUCT

Malts Springbank, Longrow & Hazelburn

Owner J & A Mitchell & Co. Ltd

Region Campbeltown

Ages Springbank 10 & 21 years old
Longrow 10 & sherry cask

Water source Crosshill Loch on the slopes of Ben Ghuilean – spring-fed and gravity-led.

Malting Uniquely it is all carried out on site on traditional malting floors. For Longrow, Optic barley from North-east Scotland is dried for 55 hours over a peat fire. For Springbank it is dried for 6 hours over peat, then over an oil-fired source for 18 hours more. For Hazelburn, due to mature first in 2007, it is dried only over the oil-fired source for 24-30 hours.

Bond There are six warehouses on site varying from traditional dunnage to modern racks seven barrels high. Visitors get to walk right in and walk down the rows. The feel and the aromas are simply divine.

Casks Ex-bourbon and sherry.

Bottling On site, but the visitor does not get to see this process. Glenfiddich is the only place in Scotland for that.

Experts' opinion 10 year old – pale, spirity, full-bodied, dry in flavour, a little oily, well balanced, with a salty tail to a smoky finish. 21 year old: positively rich, amber in colour, salty-smooth – a classic in every way. Longrow: Islay-peaty, medicinal, with a sweet smokiness. A heavy, peated malt to rival an Ardbeg – so scarce that a 'find' makes for a real red-letter day.

Our dram The miniature which your voucher procures at Eaglesomes is a no-age-given bottling of Springbank for distillery visitors – pale in colour, oily in texture, a little peppery and young but unmistakeably Springbank – balanced, a touch of peat, redolent of quality with a rich characterful aroma.

The guide, who is a former exciseman at Springbank, has a couthy style with a nice pawky wit, and an impressive grasp of his subject. There is plenty to see and every stage in the process is explained clearly and patiently. He is indefatigable on questions, and sets just the right pace. Allow an hour and more and savour it all.

Special features An embarrassment of riches – a cornucopia of distilling delights. First the maltings to see the barley steeped, spread and raked – the two maltmen turn 24 tonnes on two floors, two-and-a-half times in a 12-hour shift! Then to the kilns and a peep into the furnace with peat burning brightly with that evocative aroma. Then on to the milling room where the maroon, faded Porteous is over 150 years old. A brass plate proudly proclaims that its makers were appointed 'by Royal letters patent' – no wonder they are reputed to have gone bust through a failure to build in planned obso-lescence! The mashtun is over 100 years old, made in red-coated cast iron with a high matching under-back. Unusually it has no canopy and you climb up steps to peer into its worn but immaculate innards. The draff is reputed to keep a herd of Ayrshire cattle in the finest fettle. There are five long-serving washbacks – a fair size at 26,510 litres (5840 gallons) and coopered in knot-free Swedish larch. They look grand in their whitewashed abode with metal rafters supporting a white wood ceiling – there is a timeless, experienced air about the place. After all this excitement the three stills seem relatively small. Again, unusually, there is a feints still between the wash and the spirit still to allow for the unique two-and-a-half times distillation of Springbank and the triple distillation of the new Hazelburn (due out in 2007). All three stills are similar in shape – broad necks tapering gently to lyne arms and external con-densers. The spirit safe is longer and more complex to allow for the extra distillations, and was made by the now defunct firm of Robert Armour & Sons, Campbeltown – no doubt they flourished when there were 32 distilleries in the town. The warehouses – you really get among the barrels – complete an epic tour. Sadly, although bottling is done on site (Springbank is unique with both malting and bot-tling on site), you do not visit the bottling hall. We were assured that Springbank has no truck with caramel colouring or chill-filtering. A minor snag is that the same four men do 14 weeks of malting and then a few weeks mashing and distilling, so that you can rarely see Springbank with all guns firing at the same time. Uniquely, your tour ends in a shop!

Access This is an old distillery with lots of steps and passageways – but you see much more than almost anywhere else, with a rich tangible heritage feel to it.

Visual impact 19th-century industrial – whitewashed walls, dark corners and ancient equipment.

Range Mitchells own Eaglesomes, the famous shop in Long Row which incorporates Cadenheads, the independent bottlers of special expressions, cask whiskies and rum. Their collection is extensive, and with luck you may winkle out a bottle of Longrow – an 'almost-Islay with attitude', scarce as hen's teeth – the ultimate Graham family tipple.

Style It is, in effect, a Victorian wine merchants with chalkboards listing the specialist whiskies and rums. Your bottle will be wrapped neatly in old-fashioned wax-paper.

Staff Knowledgeable, helpful and friendly.

Catering Eaglesomes cut a mean sandwich or baguette which you can down with either their soup or coffee on the nearby seafront. For more serious trenchering the Ardsheil Hotel – inland from the ferry terminal – does excellent lunches and scrumptious dinners.

Toilets None – adjacent public conveniences only. No disabled loo. **Parent and baby** – no facilities.

Fiercely independent, Mitchells do it all for themselves and the result is two (soon to be three) outstanding malts. The tour is a no-nonsense revelation of the complete process in a setting untouched by either time or showbiz. The sheer lack of frills concentrates the mind wonderfully – the smells and aromas of malting, burning peat, washbacks and warehouse make for an unforgettable background to this definitive tour. Many visitors come to see their own cask and to renew a love affair, many more stumble upon a hidden jewel and depart infinitely richer and wiser for the experience.

Overall rating

TALISKER

Superb setting, excellent tour. Lots of tradition and a pretty stillroom. Well worth going over the sea to Skye for.

No distillery setting is more arresting. Carbost ('bost' being Norse for farm) is a small clachan on the shores of Loch Harport nestling in trees, with a pelucid burn chuckling through the grounds. Off to the seaward side lies the jetty where puffers like the *Vital Spark* (see the model in reception) landed barley and took away casks of Talisker. The buildings are neat in cream and brown, the tang of the sea is ever-present. After the visit, picnic on the shore or make for the nearby hotel in Carbost. The village and the distillery seem to co-exist in symbiotic splendour – when there's a wedding or a wake the distillery sensibly shuts down for the occasion – presumably after ample supplies of Talisker have been laid aside.

Established 1830

Enquiries 01478 640314

Website www.scotch.com

Opening hours Apr-Jun, Mon-Fri, 9am-4.30pm; Jul-Sep, Mon-Sat, 9am-4.30pm; Oct, Mon-Fri, 9am-4.30pm; Nov-Mar, Mon-Fri, 2pm-4.30pm.

Getting there Leave the main road to Portree at Sligachan and take the A863 signposted for Dunvegan. In about five miles (8km) turn left onto the B8009 to Carbost, which is partly single-track but reasonably straightforward. Follow the distillery signs.

Parking/reception Large car park immediately on the left as you reach the distillery. The visitor centre is up a flight of stairs facing the car park. Light and spacious with wood floor and ceiling, it sports gleaming 'oil' lamps and lovely flowers. The smile is friendly with a hint of Gaelic in the welcome. It is here that visitors have their dram before the

tour. While waiting, study the exquisite water colour charts, enlivened by tongue-in-cheek highland wit, which trace the distilling process.

Tour frequency Every half hour. Last tour at 4.30pm.

Maximum group size 16

Cost £3.50. Redeemable in shop. Free for under-18s.

Group bookings Write in advance to Talisker Distillery, Carbost, Isle of Skye, IV47 8SR – no coaches.

Visual aids Superb charts in the visitor centre. Multi-lingual information leaflets.

Foreign visitors Leaflet on distilling in Dutch, French, German, Italian, Spanish and Japanese. Hand boards in French, German, Italian and Spanish at each stage of the tour.

Photography in distillery? No

Disabled access Only to the stillroom floor, warehouse and shop.

THE PRODUCT

Malt   Talisker

Owner   UDV

Region   Islands

Ages   10 years old and the double-matured sherry cask edition.

Water source Fourteen underground springs that rise in Hawkhill beside the distillery.

Malting Barley is grown in the Black Isle and malted at Muir of Ord maltings. It is fairly heavily-peated.

Bond Four traditional warehouses on site in the salt air – viewing gallery with display of cooperage.

Casks White oak, ex-bourbon, used up to three times. The double-matured spends a final six months in a sherry cask. As one of the staff cultivates oysters in the loch and exports them to Spain, it looks like a fair exchange.

Bottling At Leven in Fife.

Experts' opinion A symphony of golden flavours, then a glorious lingering peat–smokiness. Spicy, smooth and almost salty at the end.

Our dram A generous straw/gold measure – mellow, peaty and smoky, lingering aftertaste of heather and sea. In a sense you get the best of Islay and the Highlands in one splendid measure. By the way, if your visit is early in the day it is worth postponing you dram until after the tour is over – the sun over the yardarm at nine in the morning can be a bit daunting!

One of the best. Well thought-out, starting with the ingredients and a view of the Porteous mill, then the 'works' in the correct logical order. The pace is gentle, the explanations clear and simple with just the right amount of detail; questions are fielded and dealt with impressively – they know their stuff here, without doubt. Although largish groups can be less than ideal, marshalling is efficient and friendly and there is space to move and to see. Microphones at key points enable the guide to be heard by all – a thoughtful touch which other distilleries might care to emulate.

Special features The mashtun, new in 1998, computer controlled and manufactured in Germany, was installed by Abercrombie of Alloa, and is resplendent in stainless steel and copper with wood trim. Two of the six Oregon-pine washbacks are newish too – all look the part (and smell it too). A feature of Talisker is a 60-hour fermentation period – most are 48 hours. The stillhouse, rebuilt after a disastrous fire in 1960, is light and spacious with five lovely lacquered copper stills – two large wash stills and three smaller spirit stills with straight, long, narrow lyne arms. Their condensers and worm tubs are outside the stillroom. Don't miss the period diagram dating from 1880 near the spirit safe. We admired the brass hatches, trimmed in red on the wash stills and blue on the spirit stills. An elegant, pine, cask-shaped spirit receiver hides to the right of the beautifully proportioned Abercrombie spirit safe.

Access Straightforward, well-planned, with nicely angled views of the stillhouse.

Range The Classic Malts range, with branded accessories.

Style Nice remake of an old building with warmth and richness. There is a stunning view of Loch Harport to be glimpsed and savoured through a tiny window behind the counter.

Staff A lovely lady who takes manifest pride in her job.

Catering None available. (Past Talisker on the right, there is a lovely shoreside picnic area.)

Toilets Immaculate. Disabled loo in the courtyard – and up a step! **Parent and baby** – no facilities.

Talisker, in the shadow of the Skye Cuillins, has a superb setting. It looks the part and has lovely people at its heart. An hour or so in their company is instructive, informative and fun – what more can you ask for? You will have travelled to a remote and spectacular spot to enjoy one of the best tours going and sample a first-class malt, part-Islay, part-Highland – you could convincingly argue that Talisker is the best of all worlds.

Overall rating

VISITED APRIL 2000 WITH MAVIS, JOHN.
AND MARGARET ALEXANDER.
BOUGHT WHISKY VERY GOOD.

TOBERMORY

Disappointing considering the setting. Tour distinctly average and welcome muted.

Splendid aspect. Tobermory claims with some justification to being the prettiest town in the Inner Hebrides with its harbour and brightly painted buildings. Visiting yachts adorn the bay while their crews visit the Mishnish Hotel famed for its ceilidhs and memories of the late Bobby McLeod, one-time owner and accordion maestro. The distillery buildings with their stout whitewashed exterior are an integral part of it all giving a pleasant courtyard aspect with views of the bay and woods. The murals on the reception walls are perhaps rather on the garish side.

Established 1798 (or was it 1823?)

Enquiries 01688 302645

Website None

Opening hours Easter-Oct, Mon-Fri, 10am-5pm; Oct-Easter, by appointment.

Getting there From the ferry terminal at Craignure on the island of Mull take the A849 to Tobermory 21 miles (33km) away. After Salen the road is single-track. Tobermory Distillery is on right as you enter the town and looks across the bay to the pier.

Parking/reception Public parking on the seafront and beyond distillery. The welcome is polite but restrained, surprisingly lacking in the anticipated highland hospitality – it gave us that 'have we come on the wrong day?' feeling. The visitor centre is rather cramped and worn-looking. We were ushered into a small ante-room and left to our own devices with a video presentation which fortunately

was rather good. The control panel was tastefully concealed in a barrel.

Tour frequency Every half-hour from 10.30am.

Maximum group size 25

Cost £2.50. Redeemable in shop.

Group bookings By appointment with the distillery office.

Visual aids 10-minute video gives pleasant views of Mull and a good, thorough description of distilling.

Foreign visitors A brochure in French but none available in English!

Photography in distillery? No

Disabled access No facilities – not recommended for the disabled.

THE PRODUCT

Malt Tobermory

Owner Burn Stewart Distillers plc

Region Island

Age 10 years old

Water source Private loch – possibly called the Misnish Lochs – water is very peaty.

Malting Malted barley comes by road and ferry from Pencaitland and Leith, – totally unpeated – the peat content of the local water suffices.

Bond On-site warehouse was sold for flats. Malt now taken to Deanston, Doune, near Stirling to rest in four 200-year-old vaults. No

salt air there which might explain why Tobermory feels more Lowland than Island.

Casks Ex-bourbon and sherry.

Bottling At East Kilbride, near Glasgow.

Experts' opinion Experts are optimistic about the future – getting more rich, expansive and smoky. With unpeated barley it has high to medium flavour, sweet overtones and a slight coffee tang with a long finish. A 20-year-old made with peated barley and sold as Ledaig can be rather splendid depending on the cask. New expressions of Ledaig are planned.

Our dram A 10-year-old Tobermory – pleasantly light and fresh – a little peaty, but nothing of the tang of the sea you expect in the islands. A reasonable but relatively anonymous dram.

This was disappointing not least because there is more than enough of interest in the distillery. Visitors are rather hustled along, and you feel that the guide has learned it all off by heart and perhaps doesn't quite understand what it is all about – I used to be that way with algebra! Answers to questions are a bit on the shaky side. It is not an easy building for large groups to move around in and as a result it is difficult to see and hear as well as one would like. The lack of a maturing ware-house (sold off as flats) does not help – perhaps a display or a model to complete the picture would give some impression of what it is like.

Special features Mashtun is cast iron, bolted in sections, with a copper canopy and an old-fashioned horizontal agitator – all rather traditional and pretty. There are four Oregon-pine wash-backs which are only part-filled, so there is no need for a switcher to break up the foam which else-where can pour over the top if fermentation is too lively. The four stills are sadly not in the best of nick and most unusually appear to be the same size. Our own investigations revealed that the wash stills are deeper 'below the waterline' – this was news to our guide! All the stills have unusually wide and steep swan necks – only the purest vapours can make it over the top! We got a good close-up view of a handsome spirit safe in action.

Access Quite demanding with a lot of steepish stairs – these and the floors which are wide 'see-through' grids can be a bit daunting if you don't like heights.

Visual impact Small, typical West Highland whitewashed stone walls. This distillery is used, rather than loved, one feels.

SHOP

Range Tobermory and Ledaig malts, Scottish Heather blend, glasses, decanters, whisky cake and rugby shirts.

Style Chaotic. Behind the counter in reception (which is small) it's a real scrum with 25 people buying and dramming as the next tour signs in.

Staff Perhaps we picked a bad day!

Catering None

Toilets None – for those caught short it is a fair sprint along the seafront to public loos!
Parent and baby – no facilities

SUMMARY

We desperately wanted to be impressed but the quality of the tour and lack of tangible warmth and commitment left us and others feeling let down. Like those who have searched for the non-existent gold bullion from the Spanish Armada rumoured to be lying in the bay, we were disappointed. With a bit of effort and some investment, things can only get better!

Overall rating

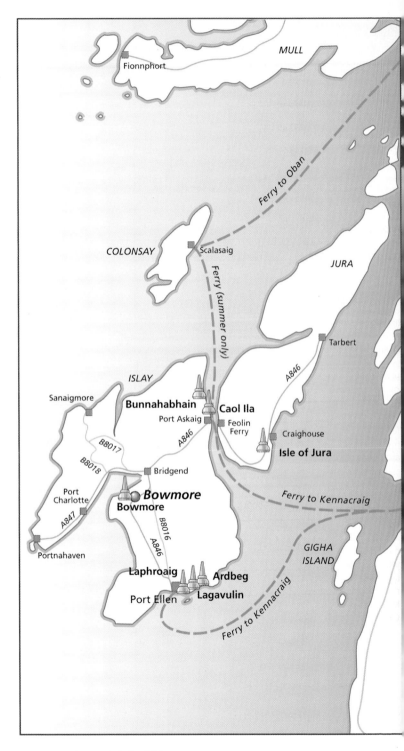

Islay & Jura

ARDBEG

BOWMORE

BUNNAHABHAIN

CAOL ILA

ISLE OF JURA

LAGAVULIN

LAPHROAIG

From the moment of boarding the ferry at Kennacraig (or in the summer at Oban on Wednesdays for an alternative route) the sheer magic of what lies ahead grips the visitor. From the gentle slopes of the South-west of Islay to the remote Paps of Jura, it is all wonderful, not just for the vistas of sea and mountain but also for the friendliness and warmth of the folks who live there – this is no idle cliché as you will find out. Where else would the visitor rate a wave from every passing car, van or distillery artic? Add no less than seven distilleries to visit and linger over and words like paradise and Valhalla spring to mind. Whether one's landfall is at Port Ellen with its sadly defunct distillery and its huge maltings, or at Port Askaig where there's barely room to park, good roads lead to distilleries where the whole is even greater than the sum of the spectacular parts. Inevitably you will want to 'do' them all.

There are lots of excellent places to stay, many of which have equally outstanding restaurants. Our favourite is the Port Charlotte Hotel (01496 850360), superbly managed by Jan and Carl Reavey with an intimate family atmosphere and first-class Scottish fare. The centrally located Bridgend Hotel (01496 810960) specialises in venison and pheasant. In Bowmore itself, try the Lochside Hotel (01496 810244) and the Harbour Inn (01496 810330) which specialises in seafood. Lunch at the Old Kiln Café at Ardbeg is not to be missed, any more than the black pudding from the local butcher in Shore Street. Don't miss a visit to C&E Roy's Celtic House – an unassuming exterior hides a cornucopia of tasteful clothes, craft goods and books. By the way, if there is anything you need to know a never failing source is the wonderful Christine Logan and her colleagues in the Bowmore Distillery visitor centre.

Crossing the water to Feolin on Jura from Port Askaig is necessary for the visit to Jura Distillery. Ferries run frequently and The Isle of Jura Hotel in Craighouse does excellent meals and bar snacks. The hotel specialises in seafood.

If you are looking for a spot to rest your head when leaving the ferry on your return from Islay, we recommend the hotel at West Loch Tarbert (01880 830930) – good for bikers too. Islay is a treat for bikes, as is the main road from Tarbert to Campbeltown on the Atlantic coast of Kintyre – a sheer winding undulating delight, and fast with it. Return via Carradale for single-track fun and awesome views of Arran.

Victorian treasure happily restored. Great for tour, views and nosh.

Ardbeg means 'small headland' in Gaelic. The setting by the shore, with rocks and reefs is idyllic and the tall buildings seem to flow naturally from the rock, all freshly white-washed since the rebirth of 1997. There are numerous nooks and crannies on the shore in which to sit and contemplate the seaward views – the staff have discreet lunchbreaks in a particularly stunning one. Ardbeg is a lovely place to visit come rain or shine. The smell of fresh baking emanating from the Old Kiln Café mingles enticingly with aromas of malt, peat, sea and spirit.

Established 1815

Enquiries 01496 302244

Website www.ardbeg.com

Opening hours All year, Mon-Fri, 10am-4pm; Jun-Sep, Mon-Sun, 10am-5pm.

Getting there From Port Ellen, take the Ardbeg road, go past Laphroaig and Lagavulin and then turn down when you see Ardbeg's silhouette below you to the right.

Parking/reception Ample parking is opposite reception. Follow the signs and once inside make for the Old Kiln Café and shop where the tour starts. You will be warmly welcomed and can pass the time before you set off with a coffee and a home-baked scone or cake. A first browse at the shop would not come amiss as there is much to see. The kiln has been beautifully renovated within its white walls and high, beamed roof. Ardbeg 'green' is much in evidence and the floors at the entrance have attractive Celtic stencils.

Tour frequency 10.30am, 11.30am, 2.30pm and 3.30pm.

Maximum group size 15

Cost £2.00. Redeemable in shop on any purchases over £15.

Group bookings Pre-booking advisable for large groups – possible to arrange tours outside set times.

Visual aids Gallery on second floor with display boards on distilling and on Islay – pretty and informative.

Foreign visitors Ardbeg – The Jewel of Islay, a history of Ardbeg and Islay is available in French, German, Spanish and Italian at £5.

Photography in distillery? Yes

Disabled access No disabled facilities.

THE PRODUCT

Malt Ardbeg

Owner Glenmorangie plc

Region Islay

Ages 10, 17 & 30 years old, 1975, 1978 and 'Provenance' at £250 a bottle.

Water source Loch Uigeadail about a mile (800m) away – soft and peaty.

Malting The highest phenolic content in the industry – over 50 ppm. Malted at Port Ellen – the barley variety is Optic.

Bond Four traditional seaside warehouses, one of which you visit – a grand sight as the first new vintage matures towards launch in 2007.

Casks Ex-bourbon with a few sherry.

Bottling Broxburn in West Lothian.

Experts' opinion Full-bodied and luscious. Big, powerful taste with an edge of richness – aftertaste has a hint of burnt Christmas cake.

Our dram The ten year old is pretty much the real Ardbeg – mercifully it is not chill-filtered and is a hefty 46% abv. The 17 is 'gentler' but with Ardbeg that is a relative term when dealing with the peatiest, saltiest, iodine-medicinal malt in the world. If you are into Islay, you must be into this one. Enthusiasts can't wait for the 'new' Ardbeg due in 2007. The guide encourages you to taste both ages, which is generous and helpful – we ended up purchasing the brace!

This is a top-level tour which can last as much as 90 minutes – but it passes in a flash. It is geared towards those who either know a bit about it or want to do so. It would be wasted on a refugee just sheltering from the rain, because it is outstanding by any standard – complete, lucid, funny and covering all the ground. It is leisurely in pace, like a family outing: by the end the guide and visitors have become a team. Marshalling is so masterfully unobtrusive. No wonder they come from continents away just to enjoy this tour. Ardbeg, famous for the peatiest, saltiest malt of them all, was closed some years ago, seemingly for ever, much to the dismay of its many admirers. In 1997 when it was bought by Glenmorangie plc it was in a sorry state. Much of the past is still there to see and as the phoenix has risen, the necessary updating has not been allowed to spoil the feel and appearance of the place. You enter the distillery through a bank of huge wooden grain bins which bear the marks of two centuries of use.

Special features The mill – a Boby of Bury St Edmunds – dates from the 1880s and was originally steam-powered. The mashtun, glorious in cast iron and painted cream with green beading, was manufactured by Newmills Ironworks of Elgin in 1961, has had its insides seen to by another Elgin firm in 1999 (a semi-lauter mechanism) and is an imposing sight. The washbacks enjoy a splendid view of Kintyre and Antrim and make an interesting contrast, three being the original larch and dark in colour, and three being new and light Oregon pine. Fermentation here takes a lengthy 60 hours. The stillroom is gloomy and old, dominated by two huge stills – heavy and 'waisted' (the spirit still most unusually is embellished by two Celtic decorative bands). Unusual features abound – both are the same size, have outside condensers and the spirit still has a 'purifier' which channels the heaviest spirit from the lyne arm back into the still for another round, as it were. The stills dwarf the spirit safe (Archibald McMillan of Edinburgh) which sits on the spirit receiver vat, a newish barrel-shaped container. Visitors actually stand on the low wines receiver and get the full benefit of the vapours, those in the know surreptitiously fingering the wet dipstick to get the best possible 'fix'.

Access Not the easiest. Ardbeg's charm is its antiquity and that means dark corners and steep stairs – better suited to the nimble.

Visual impact Terrific – a 'museum' resurrected into vitality – once mothballed and neglected, now properly used and loved. Restoration is not yet complete.

Range An unusual blend of traditional whisky wares and local crafts such as Celtic stonework and jewellery, batik, paintings and pottery. Glenmorangie and Glen Moray in their many expressions join Ardbeg on the shelves together with glasses, woollens, videos and Ardbeg nick-nacks. Overall the quality is high.

Style The kiln is spacious, whitewashed from below its pagoda roof – a pleasant setting for a well-laid out shop and cafe.

Staff Friendly, approachable – will either have been your guide, or served you coffee.

Catering The Old Kiln Café is a mecca for visitor and local alike. The homebaking is splendid, the sandwiches overflowing, the soup hot and home-made, and the daily specials bring the discerning peckish flocking from all over the Island. The steak pie is scrummy and the spiced chicken and rice a gourmet's delight. As for the clootie dumpling laced with Ardbeg, words (for once you may say) fail us! The laminated tablemats are actually old letters and bills from the archives. Browsing three tables away from our own we were eventually brought to heel by our waitress!

Toilets Modern, clean and tidy. Disabled toilet is on the ground floor adjacent to the café and shop.
Parent and baby – disabled loo is the most likely place.

Risen resplendent from its cobwebbed grave, Ardbeg has everything to commend it – a top-class tour, Victorian backdrops and a setting matched only by its neighbours at Lagavulin and Laphroaig. Don't go without planning to lunch in that delectable café. Stuart and Jackie Thomson's welcome to Ardbeg is irresistible, whether this be your first or your 40th distillery. While the tour is for the committed, anyone who joins it cannot fail to be impressed by the infectious enthusiasm of the staff.

Overall rating

BOWMORE

Superb traditional distillery, an outstanding tour. Lots of visual feasts for your eyes. Prepare to be entertained, cossetted, and refreshed liberally.

On the seafront in Bowmore, overlooking Loch Indaal, the whitewashed distillery is very much at the heart of life in the 'capital' of Islay. The views are stunning, although the wind can be snell, even in summer. A visit can be combined with a dip in the swimming pool next door (in a former distillery bond, and warmed for most of the year by distillery waste heat) and a meal at one of the town's fine hostelries.

Established 1779

Enquiries 01496 810441

Website www.bowmorescotch.com

Opening hours All year, Mon-Fri, 9am-5pm; Summer, Sat, 10am-12.30pm

Getting there If coming down Main Street, turn left at the bottom of the hill before you reach the sea. If approaching from Bridgend along Shore Street, cross Main Street. You can't miss it.

Parking/reception Entry via gates and bear right to park at the sea wall. Return to reception. Disabled visitors may park in designated spots at front entrance. Welcomes don't come any warmer than from Christine Logan and her team, Evelyn and Wilma, in their combined reception and shop. You can't miss the warmth and the sense of fun. Soon you are off to the hospitality room with its glorious views over Loch Indaal to watch an excellent video and then start your tour.

Tour frequency Winter: 10.30am and 2pm. Summer: 10.30am, 11.30am, 2pm and 3pm. Saturday: 10.30am.

Maximum group size 15

Cost £2.00. Senior citizens, £1. Redeemable in shop. Under-18s are free.

Group bookings By appointment with reception.

Visual aids The video can be shown in Italian, French, German and Spanish (videos can be bought in the shop).

Foreign visitors Some guides speak foreign languages. Good guide books in shop priced at £3.95.

Photography in distillery? Yes

Disabled access This tour is ideal for the disabled visitor – flat or gentle slopes except for a few steps to the maltings and the hospitality room – in both cases there are willing hands to assist. Blind visitors get a great welcome here.

THE PRODUCT

Malt Bowmore

Owner Morrison Bowmore Distillers Ltd

Region Islay

Ages 12, 15, 17, 21 & 30 years old. A host of special expressions as well.

Water source From the hills and via a lade from the River Laggan – peat-laden and rich.

Malting A great plus is that the visitor can see it all here as Bowmore malts 40% of its needs on the premises. The rest comes from Port Ellen Maltings.

Bond Bowmore vaults below sea level on site and others just outside Bowmore.

Casks Spanish and American oak – ex-sherry and bourbon. Double-matured has a spell in port and claret casks.

Bottling At Springburn, Glasgow.

Experts' opinion 12 year old is medium-bodied, warm and gold – smoky with heather and honey hints and a good aftertaste. Hints of chocolate and iodine.

Our dram The standard and generous dram is the 12 year old – a touch smoky with a hint of sherry, smooth but tangy – a real 'mid-Islay'. Staff let you taste any others which you might wish to buy – we fell for the 15-year-old double-matured in sherry and claret casks.

There is no better tour – comprehensive, visually arresting, well-planned and full of fascination. The commentary is witty, informed and leavened with gems of local knowledge – for example we learned that Islay House at the head of the loch has no less than 365 windows, one for every day of the year. The guides have made an art form of assessing the needs of each visitor, and vary pace and content accordingly. Working staff join in too – you get the impression that the tour has been tailor-made especially for you.

Special features Three malting floors still in use are an unusual but glorious sight, as are the kilns with peat smoke reeking forth from the pagodas – sights and aromas never to forget. After a nicely set Porteous mill, the mash house is one of the prettiest in Scotland boasting two huge 'coppers' for heating the water, a wood-encased stainless steel mashtun with a really graceful copper cover. Even the grist bin leading into the mashtun is wood-clad, complete with brass hoops. All the necessary bits are clearly labelled too – heat exchangers and underbacks etc. The computer control panel even manages to fit itself in somehow. Next along are six Oregon-pine washbacks – each named after one of the owners of Bowmore (what happens if, heaven forbid, it changes hands again?). Visitors enter the stillroom on a raised ramp which gives an excellent view of the four stills – two wash and two spirit. No two are identical, but all are handsome, single-onion jobs, sturdy and embossed with the Bowmore logo. Portholes let you see the bubbling spirits within. The stillroom is not quite big enough for all four copper condensers so one is outside in the open. Forsyth of Rothes should be proud of all four, varying in the dimensions of their swan necks and lyne arms. The spirit safe is over 100 years old, made by the long-defunct firm of Robert Armour and Sons, Campbeltown, and is polished weekly. The tour ends in the warehouse – one lucky visitor is given the key to open it. Inside it is cool, and the the air is heavy with odours that are sherry-laden. No wonder the queen has had a cask here since 1980.

Access Superb – virtually all on one level or with gentle slopes. Bright and airy.

Visual impact Stunning – no nasty industrial bits of plant to jar the eye. From the huge water kettles to the solo condenser outside, all is practical but beautiful.

Range Whiskies, books, videos, fleeces, sweatshirts, glasses, paintings, mustards and foods, flasks, golf balls, cigar cases – all high in quality and taste.

Style Spacious, open, white and dark wood, well-appointed luxury designed to loosen the purse strings – and it does.

Staff They are your guides – they'll do anything to help (well almost!).

Catering None – the Bowmore area has some great eating places close to hand. Try the Lochside Hotel for malts (over 400 in stock) and meals; the Harbour Inn for seafood and top-class porridge, and the butcher in Main Street for black pudding. Further afield, Bridgend Hotel always has game on the menu, the Loch Indaal pub in Port Charlotte has lots of malts with which to wash down good plain fare, and the Port Charlotte Hotel has an enthusiastic following for its family atmosphere, views, and excellent food – their raspberry cranachan is to die for.

Toilets Downstairs – modern, clean, sweet-smelling. Disabled loo is beside the mill and is excellent.
Parent and baby – no facilities

A superb, traditional, distillery with an outstanding tour conducted by enthusiasts with lots of lovely things to see. You can sample from a wide range of malts for every taste and leave having been entertained, educated, cossetted and well lubricated. The facilities and the care extended to disabled visitors is unsurpassed. No wonder we rated it so highly.

Overall rating NICE DVD.

VISITED 23-06-03 WITH MAVIS & BETTY
BOUGHT BOTTLE WHISKY.
PADDY

BUNNAHABHAIN

More for the dedicated enthusiast. Seldom in production and a wee bit down at heel. The stills are huge.

The approach from the A846 is spectacular with elevated views across the Sound of Islay to the Paps of Jura. The distillery is hidden away below the distillery village and is functional rather than beautiful, although the warehouses at the far end are pretty. It could do with a few picnic tables or seats from which to savour the views. The distillery buildings themselves afford few glimpses out to the Sound.

Established 1881

Enquiries 01496 840646

Website None

Opening hours Apr-Oct, Mon-Fri, 10am-4pm, by appointment only.

Getting there Take the A846 from Bowmore towards Port Askaig and turn left just after Keills at the brown sign for Bunnahabhain. After four miles (6.4km) of single-track road and superb views of the Sound of Islay, the distillery is at the end of the road. Distance markers on barrel lids mark the route.

Parking/reception Cross the cattle grid and carry on through warehouses to parking under cover on left just past the pier. Watch the pillars! Enter the green door beside the clock indicating the next tour. You will find a cosy room with displays and an invitation to help yourself to tea or coffee while you wait. Your guide, one of the working staff, will turn up on cue to welcome you and begin the tour.

Tour frequency 10.30am, 1pm and 3pm.

Maximum group size 15

Cost Free

Group bookings By appointment only via distillery office.

Visual aids Good visuals of blends, malts and maturation in reception. Some information boards on the way round.

Foreign visitors No facilities.

Photography in distillery? Yes

Disabled access No facilities available. This is not a distillery for the disabled to consider visiting.

THE PRODUCT

Malt   Bunnahabhain

Owner   Highland Distillers

Region   Islay

Age   12 years old

Water source Margadale Spring, which is not peaty, and serves the distillery village as well. Peat content is minimal – just 1ppm.

Malting Some malt is sourced from Port Ellen, some from Speyside, some from Berwick – Optima, Prisma and Chariot varieties are used.

Bond Eight warehouses on site – 22,000 casks.

Casks Ex-sherry, bourbon and refill whisky

Bottling Drumchapel, Glasgow.

Experts' opinion Medium-sweet, rich and fruity, with a touch of tar (!). A subdued smokiness with oaky tannins, smooth and creamy. An after-dinner malt.

Our dram A nice pleasant dram which is not recognisably Islay but smoother, softer and less pungent than most. Medium-sweet and fruity – more pre- than after-dinner.

There is a timeless leisure about it – well over an hour and the detail can be too much of a good thing – fascinating but verging on overload. For the real enthusiast it is a chance to get under the skin of distilling and have every question answered. Easy to hear and see, but the interiors are bit gloomy for the most part. Groups tend to be small and things are intimate and informal. Beefed up in capacity in 1961 when the Cutty Sark Blend was in peak demand, Bunnahabhain now produces for only 10-12 weeks a year (in 2000 there was no production until August) and the silent season is so long, that there is a 'mothballed' feeling in the air – it must be very frustrating for the workforce.

Special features The customary Porteous mill (dating from 1964) is followed by a gigantic mash-tun. The original cast-iron tun was replaced by a stainless steel unit in 1999. Mercifully they kept the magnificent copper canopy, with brass trim and hatches. Inside the agitator is a sturdy old horizontal job, moving on vast cogs round the perimeter. It can swallow 12-15 tonnes of grist in one gigantic mashing, disgorging the wort after four waters via a massive cooler into a vast open underback close by. The six washbacks are set high above the stillroom in splendid isolation, but are not so splendid as regards their appearance or their surroundings. Four are over 35 years old and look it, while two are newer. All six are of Oregon pine, and have curious circular iron hoops instead of flat bands. The stillroom has twin sets of wash and spirit stills, two with condensers inside the buiding and two without. They are truly massive onion shapes, with broad necks and almost horizontal lyne arms. Their impact comes from their sheer size. Two were manufactured by Lancefield Foundry and one by Blair ('Clydebuilt'), both of Glasgow. One appears to be by 'anon'. There are two spirit safes – one for each pair of stills. One is an Abercrombie (just like the old disused one at neighbour Caol Ila) and the less fancy of the two is by Lancefield Foundry. A highlight is the demonstration of casking and a visit to a classic traditional warehouse where one can see casks of all types and sizes, and nose a 1963!

Access Really difficult – steep narrow stairs, gloomy – not for the timid or the frail.

Visual impact A bit run down, and functional rather than elegant. Not pleasing to the eye, but interesting nonetheless.

Range Whisky and gin produced by the owning company, eg Black Bottle, Famous Grouse blends. Assorted branded clothing, water jugs, ice buckets, pens, umbrellas and mouse mats.

Style Up a set of stairs beside the offices, a nice Victorian feel with heavy, blue, flock wallpaper.

Staff Your guide will help – an impressive knowledge of fine whiskies and pride in their own distilling.

Catering No facilities.

Toilets Modern, clean and tidy – upstairs adjacent to shop. No disabled loo. **Parent and baby** – no facilities.

The quality of the tour is high, but slanted to those with a deep interest in malt whisky and its production. Admirers, and those who are touring all the Islay distilleries, will not miss this one. For the rest of us, it might be felt to be one of the somewhat less compelling places to visit, too often silent and a little down-at-heel. Those on their first distillery visit are advised to start elsewhere in Islay – Bowmore or one of the Port Ellen trio. Those who have a physical disability should make tracks for Bowmore.

Overall rating

VISITED 25/06/03
LOVELY SUNNY DAY

NO DRAM
BOUGHT WHISKY - BOTTLE LIQUER & POURER.

CAOL ILA

No-nonsense tour. Modern and traditional combined. The best stillroom view in Scotland.

As you drop down the winding road to the Sound of Islay, you catch a glimpse of Caol Ila below and to your left, set on a small ledge on the shore. A traditional whitewashed warehouse blends nicely with the modern buildings beyond, and from the front and the side, tantalising glimpses of the stills can be had. While the shore is less accessible than at Ardbeg or Lagavulin, the views from the stillroom defy description – especially of the Oban ferry cruising past, bound for Colonsay. If you cross to Jura, there is a path from the ferry slipway which affords views of Caol Ila from the other side.

Established 1846

Enquiries 01496 302760

Website None

Opening hours All year, by appointment, Mon-Fri. Under-8s are welcome but not encouraged to take the tour.

Getting there On the main A846 from Bowmore, take the signposted road to the left just before reaching Port Askaig. The road down is about a mile long (1.6km), single track with passing places – watch out for malt lorries.

Parking/reception Drive along the front past the warehouse: parking is on the left. Reception is on the left in the new distillery building, where you will be met by Neil and taken on tour at the appointed time. The visitor centre is new, in white and light wood, with the old pre-1973 spirit safe, restored as a working model.

Tour frequency 10am, 11.15am, 1.30pm, 2.45pm.

Maximum group size 15

Cost £3.00. Redeemable in shop.

Group bookings By appointment with visitor centre.

Visual aids The control panel in the tunroom which controls much of the process and in diagrammatic form is used to take you through things step-by-step.

Foreign visitors Leaflets in Dutch, French, German, Italian, Japanese and Spanish

Photography in distillery? Yes

Disabled access Modern and well-lit, but stairs make it difficult for those in wheelchairs.

THE PRODUCT

Malt Caol Ila

Owner UDV

Region Islay

Age 15 years old

Water source Loch nam Ban, a mile (1.6km) away in the hills above the Sound.

Malting At Port Ellen. Less peaty content than many Islay malts.

Bond Warehouses for malt whisky maturation are on site – traditional, three storeys. Not visited on the tour.

Casks Mainly refill whisky casks and ex-bourbon.

Bottling Glasgow

Experts' opinion Delicate nose, Islay characteristics, medium in its properties, but still smoky and agreeably pungent, with bitter chocolate and spice traces. A great after-dinner dram.

Our dram A generous measure of the 15 year old. It is unmistakeably Islay, but less peaty and 'in your face' than some. It is lovely, rounded, smooth, with plenty of character. Pity most of it goes for blending.

This is an excellent tour made by the fact that the guide, Neil, has worked at the distillery for 30 odd years, built the washbacks, and distilled your dram. The pace is comfortable, the views are good, and the marshalling unobtrusive. Quiet humour allied to depth of knowledge makes every query a source of interest and enlightenment. The modern technique for cleaning washbacks is demonstrated with feeling by a man who used to do it the hard way from the inside.

Special features The distillery was rebuilt in 1973-4 and is modern in style with plenty of windows and space. Although the roof is corrugated iron, all the essentials are traditional, and attractively laid out. After visiting the Porteous mill (one of the few things to survive the rebuild), visitors ascend to the combined mash and tun room to be confronted with one of the biggest mash-tuns in the business – it takes 11.5 tonnes of grist and is 22ft (6.7m) across. Made of cast iron, it is cream-painted with an exquisite copper lid with brass hatches and beading. Inside is a mammoth agitator to stir the 'porridge'. Like the stills it was built by Abercrombie of Alloa. The heat-exchanger is a real cracker – claimed to be made with the same materials as a spaceship but looked more like an old car radiator to us! The eight sizeable washbacks were built on site by Neil and his colleagues ('muscles like Arnie Schwarzenegger when we were done!') and are of Finnish pine. They have trim chocolate-coloured tops and five yellow hoops, and Neil tells visitors proudly that they have never leaked a drop. The grated floor here is wide, enabling the visitor to appreciate their full depth. Next down to the stillroom – a dramatic sight with its wall of windows overlooking the Sound and its six, tall, elegant, slender onion stills, each with a condenser behind. The wash stills have red hatch trims, and the spirit have blue. Broad-necked and with gently sloping lyne arms this is a sight of some grandeur – each glowing golden-red. Two fine spirit safes dating from the rebuild of 1973 are modern-looking and smooth (Abercrombie). Close by is a handsome oak spirit receiver.

Access Easy – spacious, brightly painted and well-lit. Two storeys of broad stairs.

Visual impact A modern distillery rebuilt in the early 1970s, but with traditional mash and still-rooms. It is similar to those at Aberfeldy and Clynelish but has the best stillroom view in Scotland – over the Sound of Islay and the Paps of Jura.

SHOP

Range Whisky, glasses, decanters, and branded polo shirts. Limited expression bottlings.

Style Low-key, nicely laid out – understated.

Staff Your guide and the ladies from reception – as always the warm Islay manner is in evidence.

Catering None – but the Port Askaig Hotel Bridgend Hotels are not too far away.

Toilets New and spotless as are those for the disabled in the visitor centre. **Parent and baby** – no facilities available.

SUMMARY

This is a straightforward no-nonsense tour of a modern distillery which has succeeded in keeping its traditions and character. Like the lovely malt it distils, it is sometimes underrated in the Islay pecking order but if you visit here, you will see how wrong they are. A good 'from the horse's-mouth' tour, a pleasant shop and visitor centre, and the views of the stills and of the Paps – all these combine to make it a memorable occasion. Caol Ila (pronounced Kull-eela by the way) is worth going out of your way for.

Overall rating

VISITED 25/06/03
BOUGHT WHISKY. LOVELY DRAM
MAVIS BOUGHT JOHNS BIRTHDAY BOTTLE.

ISLE OF JURA

Innards robust rather than pretty with stills 27ft/8.2m high. A warm welcome and a tour of pure unvarnished gold set in an island of exquisite charm.

On a fine day Jura is the place to be with its beauty subtly enhanced by its remoteness and an air of mystery. One can appreciate how George Orwell managed to pen *1984* a few miles up the road at Barnhill. The distillery stands in the middle of the settlement of Craighouse, where the steamer used to call, with palm trees across the road to emphasise its sheltered aspect. The buildings make an odd mix – built in 1810, dismantled in pique in 1908, restored in a fairly utilitarian manner in 1963 and again when two extra stills were added in 1978. Workmanlike rather than pretty, its history and its setting add a certain robust charm – amply compensating for the effort of getting there.

Established c1810 rebuilt 1960-3

Enquiries 01496 820240

Website None

Opening hours All year, by appointment only; Mon-Thu, 9am-4pm; Fri, 9am-1pm.

Getting there From Port Askaig, Islay, take the ferry to Feolin (5 minutes, about £12 return for car and two people) across the Sound of Islay. Follow the only single-track road for 6 miles (9.6km) to Craighouse – you can't miss the distillery on your left.

Parking/reception Find your own spot round about – there is no car park as such. (A new visitor centre opens in May 2001.) Make for the office in the low building in front, where the roses bloom in summer. A real Jura welcome awaits and your tour guide will be one of the staff – in our case Willie, the brewer. The emphasis is on intimate informality.

Tour frequency 10.30-11ish, 2pm or by mutual discussion.

Maximum group size 15

Cost Free

Group bookings By appointment with distillery office.

Visual aids Good diagrams in reception.

Foreign visitors No special facilities

Photography in distillery? Yes, but not in the stillroom and filling store.

Disabled access The distillery is not geared to lots of visitors and is fairly inaccessible. Even so, staff will do all to help – the stillroom and cask filling are within reach.

THE PRODUCT

Malt   Isle of Jura

Owner   JBB (Greater Europe) plc

Region   Island

Ages   10, 16 & 21 years old

Water source Market Loch (so called as it was on the drove route from Islay to Kintyre. The peatiness of the Jura malt whisky comes from the water only.

Malting Unpeated, from Port Ellen in Islay or Simpsons of Berwick.

Bond Five warehouses on site – eight racks high – 27,000 casks.

Casks Refill whisky

Bottling At Leith, the port of Edinburgh.

Experts' opinion Subtle peaty traces, well-matured but delicate. Good body, soft and smooth. Lingering quality to the aftertaste. Some good herbal and floral aspects. Good pre- and post-prandial tipple.

Our dram We were able to sample generous nips of the 16 and 21 year old – great hospitality and easy on the palate. Both are delicate, slightly peaty, and smooth. The 21 year old has extra sherry overtones. A nice mix of Highland and Island.

Authentic shop-floor stuff, but tempered to suit the needs of each group – either in-depth or just the main points. Nice pace, humour, and anecdote – visitors are guaranteed to learn and to enjoy. Marshalling is gentle and there is space to see at all the key points.

Special features The tour starts where the casks arrive and are filled – dampness is an asset here as anyone who has a wooden boat will appreciate. Pebble floors and whitewash are the order of the day. Next the mashtun – a huge stainless steel semi-lauter installed in the late 1970s, replacing a cast-iron item, whose beautiful copper lid now graces the mashtun at Bowmore. The new one is big and functional, just like the six immense stainless steel washbacks – unusually it takes two mashes to fill each one – with 48,900 litres (10,771 gallons) of wort precisely! Remember to take a look over to the islands and distant Kintyre from here. Fermentation takes a relatively leisurely 59 hours before the wash passes to four splendidly statuesque stills which are no less than 27ft/8.2m high with broad necks and gently sloping lyne arms. When MacMillan of Prestonpans manufactured the stills in 1963 and 1978 they made them in two halves which were then bolted together on site with brass collars. They are severely 'waisted' – this directs the heavy spirit vapour (which does not make it over the top and condenses as it drops back) into the very middle of the distilling wash and low wines for re-distilling. With this and the sheer height of the stills (the highest there are), the resultant spirit is light, dry and oily. The spirit safe is massive, serving both sets of stills, and is business-like and sturdy if less elegant than some. The tour concludes with cask filling and then the generous dram.

Access Not the easiest, with some steepish stairs, but no great problems for most folk.

Visual impact Very much working and bigger than you expect if you are thinking, as we were, of a tiny, out-of-the-way cottage distillery.

Range Isle of Jura whisky, and other owner-company whiskies, glasses and quality branded fleeces (reversible to cope with the changeable weather) – a real snip at £25.00 – we bought two!

Style Small, intimate and in keeping with the feel of the place.

Staff Our guide or even the distillery manager himself.

Catering None, but try the adjacent Jura Hotel for meals and malts. At lunchtime there is a fine range of home-made fare – start with the piping hot soup. The view from the intimate bar over Small Isles bay is pleasant.

Toilets Modern (new in 2001). No disabled loo. **Parent and baby** – no facilities available.

The warmth of the welcome, the romance, and the history of Jura Distillery somehow more than make up for the fact that its working innards are robust, rather than pretty (it was rebuilt by brewers, after all). Jura malt pilgrims will make light of the journey. You should too. The tour is pure unvarnished gold, and the drams generous. The combined experience of visiting Jura and its distillery is what really makes this worth the effort.

Overall rating

VISITED 26.06.03 WITH MAVIS BETTY AND PADDY.
LOVELY SUNNY DAY GREAT VIEWS
NICE DRAM - 10 YEAR OLD

LAGAVULIN

Timeless tradition, a legendary malt, and a glorious setting. A first-class no-nonsense-tour and a superb copper-filled stillroom.

In a little bay with the Island of Texa just offshore, Lagavulin's setting could not be finer. Before the advent of the roll-on – roll-off ferries, puffers crept past the headland on which stands the remains of 13th-century Dunyvaig Castle and nudged alongside the jetty to unload barley and take the finished product to the mainland. The distillery buildings stand on the shore, white and roughcast, tall and proud, with two distinctive pagodas, sadly no longer in use. The legend 'Lagavulin' on the walls can be seen from miles away by passing fishermen and yachties alike.

Established 1816

Enquiries 01496 302400

Website www.scotch.com

Opening hours All year, Mon-Fri. Visits by appointment only. If the staff are free, weekend visits might be possible

Getting there From Port Ellen take the Ardbeg road. Lagavulin is the second distillery on the right – on the roadside in a couple of miles.

Parking/reception On the right, immediately before the distillery. A great Islay welcome from Marjorie the guide. The offices, reception and dram room are all wood-panelled in a tasteful manner – soft green and cream – a very Scottish period feel, cool and relaxing. A huge quilt map of Islay in reception is worth a closer look.

Tour frequency 10am, 11.30am and 2.30pm.

Maximum group size 14

Cost £3.00. Redeemable in shop.

Group bookings Like all visits, by appointment only.

Visual aids None, but you can taste malted barley and smell the seaweed and the peat.

Foreign visitors Leaflets in Dutch, French, German, Italian, Japanese and Spanish.

Photography in distillery? Yes

Disabled access There is a hoist to reception, the stillroom can be reached with some difficulty, the cask filling easily but the rest is not a practical proposition.

THE PRODUCT

Malt Lagavulin

Owner UDV

Region Islay

Ages 16 years and double-matured in ex-sherry casks.

Water source Exclusive to Lagavulin is the peaty water of the Solan Lochs. You can see just how peaty it is by looking at the burn beside the distillery.

Malting A variety of barley such as Optic, grown in East Lothian or Aberdeenshire and malted at the maltings in Port Ellen – 20 times peatier than a Speyside.

Bond At Lagavulin, Port Ellen and Caol Ila. Not part of the regular tour, but if they are

open, Marjorie will show you round.

Casks Mainly ex-bourbon, some ex-sherry and refill whisky.

Bottling At Leven in Fife.

Experts' opinion 'Waves of dark-brown iodine-rich, seaweedy flavour which crash like breakers on the palate,' robust, full-bodied, with a well-balanced, smooth, lingering finish. 'Time takes out the fire, but leaves the warmth.'

Our dram We're biased – we love Islay malts. This is the bestseller of all of them and deservedly so – at 16 years, it is peaty, salty, smoky, heavy – 'rare a'thegither'. Some folk have to work their way up to the Islay malts, but the rewards are great! A sophisticated alternative is the double-matured Lagavulin – redolent of sherry sweetness.

This is a working distillery, its product in great demand, and there are always staff on hand to add to Marjorie's considerable knowledge, should that prove necessary. This is a first-class, no-nonsense tour of leisurely ambulatory discussion. By the end of it, you will have fallen for the magic of the place. The views are good, the planning immaculate and the cask-filling with Ian (a star in his own right) a fitting climax.

Special features The tour starts with the mill – a maroon Porteous dating from 1963 and then on to a 4.5-tonne capacity mashtun, fashioned in stainless steel, with a hatched lid. On to no less than 10 washbacks, all over 50 years old, made of dark New England larch, and with smart unvarnished pine lids, all new in 2000. A computer programme reveals at which stage in the long 55-75 hour cycle each washback is, enabling us to trace the process from filling to foaming out. After that the wash is ready for distillation. The stills (two wash, two spirit) are 'working' rather than cosmetic – but are a glorious pear-shape, unique to Lagavulin, with copper condensers behind. The wash stills have a pronounced curve at the swan-neck and the lyne arm is at quite an angle. The second distillation takes all of ten hours, more of a simmer than a boil to keep the flavour in. There are glorious copper pipes everywhere, and a brass spirit safe (like the stills, made by Abercrombie of Alloa) sits atop the feints and low wines receiver. Close by is a 23,000-litre (5066-gallon) Oregon-pine spirit receiver. By lifting the dipstick and nosing it you can smell the smoke and peat in the spirit. The padlock on the safe is the massive original – it still has an indent for the exciseman's paper seal.

Access Fairly straightforward, with a good few steps, but bright and fresh.

Visual impact Working it may be, but worn it is not, a nice 'farm' feel and traditional things to delight the eye.

Range Lagavulin and Classic Malts range, coasters, glasses, flasks.

Style On the counter at reception – small and typically intimate.

Staff Majorie again, or even the distillery manager himself.

Catering None – Port Ellen has hotels and there is a super café/restaurant at the 'next along' distillery which is Ardbeg.

Toilets Lovely, clean and perfumed – in wood to match the rest of the decor. Disabled loo in reception. **Parent and baby** – no facilities.

Timeless tradition, a magic end-product, and a setting to die for, Lagavulin's charms are irresistible. It is a no-frills, working distillery which opens its heart to you, and then reveals some, if not all of its secrets. The tour is one of the best around – no gimmicks, just a deep, dedicated knowledge and a feast for the eye to boot. When everything turns pear-shaped, just pray that it will be like the stills of Lagavulin.

Overall rating

LAPHROAIG

Peat-smoke from the kilns, an excellent tour including the malting floors and seven lovely stills. Little wonder such a peaty, smoky masterpiece is made here.

After the vast expanse of the 10 miles (16km) of the Laggan Moss from Bowmore to Port Ellen with its huge maltings dwarfing the sadly defunct Port Ellen Distillery, it is a relief to take the bonnie three-mile (4.8km) coast road to Ardbeg, with its three famous distilleries. Laphroaig is the first, and like the others is whitewash-walled, set on the rocky coastline and looks every inch the part, not least because peatreek still pours from its twin pagodas. Neat, tidy, with traditional farmhouse buildings, it fulfils all the visitors' expectations. This is where one of the great 'character' whiskies of the world is distilled and matured, and you can see for yourself.

Established 1826

Enquiries 01496 302418

Website www.laphroaig.com

Opening hours All year, by appointment only. Silent season usually is Jul-Aug. Join the Friends of Laphroaig and get a square foot of Islay to own, and your name inscribed in a book of many volumes. When you visit you get paid 'rent' in the shape of a miniature.

Getting there Take the Ardbeg road from Port Ellen, Laphroaig is the first of the three distilleries along a lovely coastal road. It is down a short drive on the seaward side.

Parking/reception A place of few signposts: bear right at the end of the avenue into the distillery and sharp left to the car park. Up the external stairs to sign in, and then across to the dram room which has lovely views, but needs a bit of 'tlc'. Your guide (sometimes a member of staff) will meet you and the tour starts in the malt barns.

Tour frequency 10.15am and 2.15pm.

Maximum group size 15

Cost Free.

Group bookings Like all visits, by appointment only.

Visual aids Boards in key areas give good clear information. There are excellent leaflets on the history and distilling of whisky in the dram room.

Foreign visitors No special provisions

Photography in distillery? Yes

Disabled access Not the easiest of tours for the disabled but assistance is available. If this is a critical issue for you, Bowmore is a better bet.

THE PRODUCT

Malt   Laphroaig

Owner   Allied Distillers

Region   Islay

Ages   10, 15 & 30 years old.

Water source Kilbride Dam – lots of peat and heather.

Malting 30% from the malting floors at Laphroaig, 70% from Port Ellen Maltings. The variety is Optic and the source is EU.

Bond Eight warehouses on site

Casks Largely ex-bourbon hogsheads, from Kentucky, USA.

Bottling Dumbarton, on the north bank of the River Clyde.

Experts' opinion Amber-coloured with a heavy peat-smoke aroma. Full of character, full-bodied with a hint of sherry as well as an iodine/medicinal tinge. Finish is long, smoky and refined. Can it be true that the medicinal elements allowed it to be prescribed by American doctors during Prohibition?

Our dram The 10 year old we sampled is pungent, peaty and a bit untamed. Some say that the chilling process before bottling has taken the edge off it and that might be so. It once was bottled at 43%, but no longer. The five years extra slumber in warehouses close to the sea air really lifts the 15 year old – fuller, smoother, and richer.

The tour is one of substance and quality, covering all the main features (except the warehouses) and is straightforward, easy to follow, and almost uniquely enables the visitor to see malting in process. Apart from Bowmore on Islay, and Springbank in Campbeltown, you may have to go to Orkney to see a similar sight. Questions are fully answered and the 'working' guides really know their stuff. There is a fair bit of climbing and descending, but marshalling is good and stopping points afford good views.

Special features The high point comes first. Here you can see barley being malted on two huge floors – laid out from 'chariots', raked, turned, nurtured and then dried in peatreek from sods cut from the Glen Machrie bog. On to the two kilns with traditional pagoda roofs – take it from us, this is worth the visit alone: the sights, the sweat, the smells, the reek – glorious. Strangely after this traditional start, the next stage is a bit stark and mechanistic. Previous owners Whitbread had a hand in things in the 1970s and 80s and it shows in some clear 'brewery' features – the Porteous mill is 60 years old and came from a London brewery, the mashtun installed in 1984 is best described as efficient – the six stainless steel washbacks, totally enclosed and just a year younger, may be easy to clean, but they are not easy on the eye – how one yearns for a bit of wood, copper or brass to lighten the steel jungle of pipes and vessels. Fortunately the stillroom more than makes up for it. It is bright with big windows, and a positive regiment of gleaming stills, three wash and four spirit all in a row, resplendent in copper, with shapely condensers behind. They are 'nipped' in at the waist, elegantly proportioned, with a narrow neck and long, thin, lyne arms on the wash stills which most unusually slope up at a pronounced angle. The stills were built by Macdonald of Edinburgh and have been refettled by Forsyth from Rothes. An inspection of casks and casking in the restored 1860's farm buildings rounds off a thorough, comprehensive experience – we even got the chance dip our fingers in the spillage to smell the peat in the spirit.

Access A bit awkward at times – the price of seeing the malting floors and kilns. Stairs can be steep and it can be a bit dark. OK with care.

Visual impact In the mash and tun rooms there is too much steel and pipework to charm, but the mill, the stillhouse and the cask-filling largely compensate.

Range Laphroaig whiskies and assorted products – a video about the distillery, books, glasses, decanters, branded clothing, sweat shirts, jumpers, hats – all of high quality.

Style Behind the bar in the dram room – malts to mouse mats!

Staff Shop opened up by your tour guide – friendly, knowledgeable, helpful.

Catering None

Toilets Modern with a high level of cleanliness. Disabled loos are modern and clean. **Parent and baby** – no facilities.

A visit to Laphroaig has much to commend it. Laphroaig set the standard for bottled Islay malts, it still malts some of its own barley and it has a setting second to none. The tour is thorough and well-researched, the stillroom a delight, and the smell of peat and smoke is evocative in the extreme. The mash and tun rooms dilute the mystique a little and the dram room and shop could do with a bit of a makeover, but these are small reservations when set against the overall quality of the experience.

Overall rating

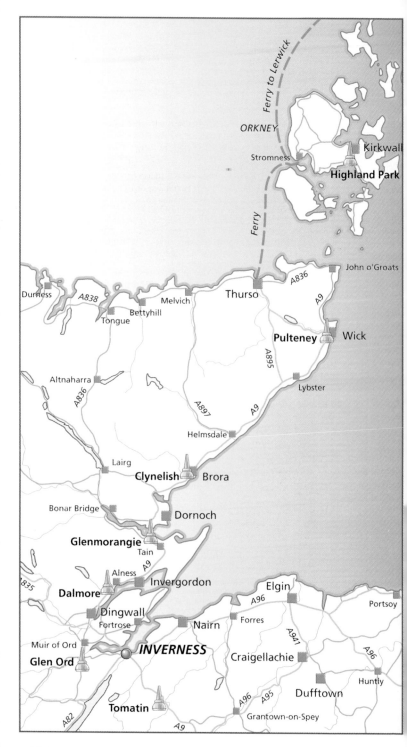

Ferry to Lerwick

ORKNEY

Stromness

Kirkwall

Highland Park

John o'Groats

A836

Durness

A838

Melvich

Thurso

A9

Bettyhill

Tongue

Pulteney

Wick

A895

Altnaharra

A9

Lybster

A836

A897

Helmsdale

Lairg

Clynelish

Brora

Bonar Bridge

Dornoch

Glenmorangie

Tain

A9

Dalmore

Alness

Dalmore

Invergordon

Elgin

A96

Dingwall

Portsoy

A835

Fortrose

Nairn

Forres

Muir of Ord

A941

INVERNESS

Craigellachie

A96

Glen Ord

Huntly

Dufftown

A82

Tomatin

A96

A95

A9

Grantown-on-Spey

Orkney & The North of Scotland

TOURING CENTRE: INVERNESS

There is no obvious centre for this area. Inverness is more of a starting and finishing point: Muir of Ord, Brora or Thurso would serve just as well, not to mention Stromness, or Kirkwall when visiting Highland Park in Orkney. The three most northerly of the seven distilleries in this group (Highland Park in Orkney, Pulteney in Wick and Clynelish outside Brora) can all be conveniently reached from Thurso or Wick. In Thurso comfortable accommodation is available at the St Clair Hotel (01847 896481) and you can have an excellent seafood meal in the Upper Deck at Scrabster overlooking the harbour and the ferry terminal.

Should you decide to stay overnight or longer in Orkney, then you could do no better than at the Ferry Inn in Stromness for cosy accommodation and hearty fare – the best lobster thermidor that ever paved the way for a dram of Highland Park Bicentennial. While in Orkney make sure and visit the 5000-year-old village at Skara Brae and wonder at the contrast between St Magnus Cathedral in Kirkwall and the Italian Chapel in a former Nissen hut overlooking the Churchill causeways on Scapa Flow. The best way to see and sample the many islands is to take the special Sunday-only trip from Kirkwall organised by the Orkney Shipping Company.

Further south, while visiting the other distilleries in the region, Glenmorangie near Tain, Dalmore on the shore of the Cromarty Firth near Alness, Glen Ord at Muir of Ord, or Tomatin on the A9, some 16 miles (26km) south of Inverness, you could do very much worse than the superb b&b provided by Catherine Peterkin at Hillview Park in Muir of Ord (01463 870787). On a balmy evening combine it with wonderful fish'n'chips from Beauly, eaten al fresco in the square.

The Caravan Club have a first-class site at Dalchalm just above Brora, and a less exciting one at Riverside, Wick. Another great centre is the Camping and Caravanning Club site at Dingwall.

CLYNELISH

DALMORE

GLENMORANGIE

GLEN ORD

HIGHLAND PARK

PULTENEY

TOMATIN

Standard tour of modern distillery. The warehouses of the old Brora Distillery are interesting

The old and the new blend well with this modern distillery on a grassy knoll overlooking the dark stone of its old counterpart, still complete with a pagoda. The views of the hills and the sea are delightful. Flower beds and a picnic table adorn the immediate environment. A great place to be on a summer's day with a visit to Brora's tiny harbour is an essential part of the experience.

Established 1819

Enquiries 01408 623000

Website www.highlandescape.com

Opening hours Mar-Oct, Mon-Fri, 9.30am-5pm.

Getting there Off the main A9 just north of Brora – follow the signs up the Balnacoil Road. The new distillery is about a quarter of a mile (400m) away on the hillside.

Parking/reception Up the drive and circle left to the car park signposted at the side of the distillery. This is behind the new (1967) distillery. Visitors pay in the shop then wait next door in in a warm reception room, with tartan curtains and Danish pine 'barrels' to recline in while you watch the sheep 'out the back'.

Tour frequency Every half-hour.

Maximum group size 15

Cost £3.00. Redeemable in shop.

Group bookings By appointment with reception.

Visual aids None, but the main constituent parts are clearly labelled.

Foreign visitors Translations about the process are available in Czech, Italian and French. In addition there is a German-speaking guide.

Photography in distillery? Yes

Disabled access Whilst access is good to the shop and visitor centre, access to the distillery is not possible. Staff indicate that they make no special provision.

THE PRODUCT

Malt Clynelish

Owner UDV

Region Highland (northern)

Ages 14 years and 24 year-old cask-strength

Water source Clynemilton Burn – claimed to run over veins of gold on its way down the mountain.

Malting From Glen Ord Maltings in Muir of Ord. 70% of the barley is Scottish. Moderately peated.

Bond Three traditional dunnage warehouses on site – only 5% of production is stored on site for Clynelish 14 year old. Spirit for blends

is stored in Central Scotland. The excellent Brora malt (only a little of it is left) is here too.

Casks Ex-bourbon and sherry.

Bottling Leven in Fife

Experts' opinion Peaty for a Northern malt, with a pleasant but dry finish. Fruity flavour comes through; it is somewhat overshadowed by Brora which deprives it of its full stature. The 21-year-old Brora is now £60 a bottle and there is not a lot of it left.

Our dram A little parsimonious in quantity, but warm, smooth, soft, smoky, full-bodied and sweet. More body than its light colour would suggest. Not as characterful by a long chalk as the peaty Brora of the past, but it has its own cachet.

An average, standard tour covering the main points of the process clearly and in sequence, with a fair opportunity for questions. It is difficult to avoid an impression that it is all a little hurried and perfunctory. With a modern mash and tun room set above a picture-window stillroom, the logistics are easy but hearing what is said can be difficult at times. Marshalling is unsubtle with pressure to keep up or get left behind.

Special features The 'new' Clynelish was built in 1967 to a standard design. The old distillery close by continued to make the peaty Brora until 1983. Clynelish looks a bit boxy but it is bright, cream-walled, with plenty of windows from which to view the sea and hills. The mashtun is fairly large with a 12.5-tonne capacity and is made of white-painted cast iron with a splendid copper canopy and brass-trimmed hatches. A large, open, steel underback gives an opportunity to smell the hot wort before it passes through an Alfa-Laval heat exchanger. In the same first-floor hall are eight Oregon-pine washbacks dating back to 1967. Being dark in colour they look a little sombre with their broad black hoops. In the tops of them are glass viewing hatches – the view is excellent, but the magic aromas are, as a result, sadly emasculated. The stillroom below is impressive – six massive stills in a row – the wash stills with red hatches and pipework, the spirit stills in blue. The stills taper to straight lyne arms leading to copper condensers. As at Coal Ila and Aberfeldy, visitors pass under the lyne arms between the stills and the condensers. Like the two spirit safes – a small one for low wines and a larger one for spirit, they are the work of Abercrombie of Alloa. The safes are set on wooden plinths, adorned with still-shaped carvings. Nearby is a dark, oak, spirit receiver from which an overhead pipe takes the spirit to the filling room in the old distillery. A brief visit to a fine old warehouse dating from 1896 to see casks of Clynelish and Brora, stacked two high in a cool, stone-walled environment, completes the tour. An undue uptake of the angels' share in the past led to some suspicion that enterprising workers had dug their own tunnel into Brora Distillery. Sadly their endeavour was not appreciated by the management!

Access Excellent – modern, bright, well-lit, with good stairs and wide passages.

Visual impact As at Aberfeldy and Caol Ila, the former owners (Scottish Malt Distillers) have contrived to create a modern building with satisfying traditional innards. Attractive, bright, with bonnie views from the windows.

Range Clynelish and Brora malts, Johnnie Walker Black Label, glasses, Pringle knitwear and polo shirts.

Style Low key – limited range but all the expected items are present.

Staff Welcoming and friendly.

Catering None

Toilets Excellent facilities in the well-appointed visitor lounge. Toilet facilities for the disabled are available in the visitor centre. **Parent and baby** – no facilities.

A standard tour which provides a good beginners' guide to the distilling process, with attractive bright mashtun and stillrooms. The setting is pleasant as is the warehouse atmosphere – more could be made of this. Whether it's the brooding presence of the neglected home of the wonderful Brora next door, or the efficient but uncommitted air of the guides, it is not as uplifting a place to visit as it could be.

Overall rating

DALMORE

They come no better than this. Prepare to devote time and enjoy the perfect tour. A feast for eye and nose. Book now!

Set right on the shore with oystercatchers and herons moving in with the rising tide, this is a wonderful, relaxed setting. The grey stone buildings are not individually handsome, but collectively they are pleasing. Close by is the Yankee Pier, built by American servicemen who made mines at Dalmore during the First World War. This is a fitting setting for dedicated folk distilling a classic malt. Ranks with Caol Ila on Islay for scenic views.

Established 1839

Enquiries 01349 882362

Website None

Opening hours By appointment only.

Getting there Leave the A9 just north of Alness on to the B817. At a T-junction turn left for Invergordon. The entrance to Dalmore is on your right. Go down a winding leafy drive until you reach the shore of the Cromarty Firth – then turn left.

Parking/reception Parking is on either side beyond the office buildings. Each visit is individually arranged. Visitors climb the stairs to the office, with its lovely gold-embossed lettering on the door, where a friendly welcome awaits and your guide, very often assistant manager Drew Sinclair, is introduced. After a chat in the beautiful hospitality room with its lovely period furniture, pictures, fireplace and views, your tour begins.

Tour frequency As arranged.

Maximum group size 20

Cost Free

Group bookings Must be arranged prior to visit.

Visual aids None – apart from the many eyecatching features on the tour, that is.

Foreign visitors No special provision.

Photography in distillery? Yes

Disabled access The milling room, stillroom and warehouse are accessible.

THE PRODUCT

Malt The Dalmore

Owner JBB (Greater Europe) plc

Region Highland (northern)

Age 12 years old

Water source The River Averon (Alness) which flows from Loch Kilmorie.

Malting Lightly peated and malted at Baird's Maltings, Inverness – usually Optic variety.

Bond Ten warehouses on site – mainly traditional dunnage, racked three casks high. Visitors can penetrate deep inside to see a wide variety of casks from Dalmore as well as casks for blends from other distilleries.

Casks Ex-sherry, bourbon and refill whisky.

Bottling At Leith, Edinburgh.

Experts' opinion A medium- to full-bodied, velvety malt with a deep mahogany glow – a mellow quality adds to its polished intense bouquet. The sherry taste lingers long. Full of honey, beautifully balanced – more lush and muscular than it used to be, and all the better for that.

Our dram A generous dram is dispensed in the elegant lounge by your guide and you may well meet the manager too. A sip immediately confirms that Dalmore's distilling features result in a unique, characterful malt which is the match of any – distinctive, rich, mellow and smooth with a lovely dark colour. 'Smooth' meaning – in this context – very, very, smooth. The aftertaste lingers on and on. An after-dinner treat.

It is difficult to avoid superlatives here. What you get is an individual, privileged, insight into the life and history of a fascinating distillery from a man who has lived and breathed Dalmore for more than 30 years. You are not shepherded ... you are cossetted. There are forays to see hidden gems such as disused steam engines and a vintage lorry along the way. This is as thorough and compelling a tour as you will find anywhere in Scotland – bar none. Tearing yourself away is the biggest problem you will face.

Special features A new mashhouse was built in 1991 and at the same time a new mill was installed – as ever by Porteous of Hull, but now linked with the name of Richard Sizer. Visitors can witness the entire milling process from dressing to grist. The mashhouse, lined in yellow brick, while modern, is perfectly in keeping and holds a fairly large semi-lauter mashtun (9.2-tonne grist capacity). It is stainless steel with a fetching peaked canopy which catches the sun through attractive roof lights. The draff is deposited outside and is then blown up a bank for loading into lorries. The pipe used for this is scoured by blowing a size-5 football through it! Close by is a disused underback in black-painted cast iron with red tooling. Next door the original tun room houses eight Oregon-pine washbacks dating from 1953 to the 1980s. Cream walls and corrugated roofs give a lovely 'farm' feel and there are tantalising vistas of the Cromarty Firth and sundry mothballed oil platforms from the narrow windows. The washbacks were once cleaned with lime, brushed on with heather besoms (brooms) made by the men. Unique in our experience is a huge pine wash charger – at least 20ft/6m across, with two paddles that used to agitate the wash and ensure that sediment did not enter the stills first. The operator walked round with a huge tiller – reminiscent of winding lock gates on a canal. The single stillhouse was once two, with the burn flowing in between. Now it houses no less than eight stills, four at each end paired as wash and spirit – again a unique arrangement. These stills abound in remarkable features: for a start they are chunky with the spirit stills having a more pronounced mini double-onion, and remarkably they have flat tops with the massive lyne arms connected just below them. The spirit stills have copper jackets to cool and condense alcohol which has not made it over the top so that it can be redistilled. At least one of these jackets dates from 1870, and was the work of Anderson & Dickson of Edinburgh, long since out of business. The condensers are outside, the ones for the wash stills conventionally vertical, the spirit ones horizontal. Make no mistake, these are unconventional pieces of plant. The stills bear the mark of McMillan, but are now in the hands of Forsyth of Rothes. There are no less than four spirit safes – three handsome and fairly conventional, and one of great antiquity with brass vents above and circular brass knobs for controlling the flow of spirit. Half-a-level down are three Oregon-pine spirit receivers. Then on to the warehouse, via the filling room to see casks charged with new spirit.

Access Superb – virtually all on one level or with gentle slopes. Bright and airy.

Visual impact Stunning – ancient waterwheels, the aforesaid steam engine, stills of unique character, no less than four spirit safes. A feast for the eye and the nose.

Range There is no shop: ironically the distillery has no licence to retail whisky. You must buy your Dalmore elsewhere – but after trying it, you will.

Toilets Available in the office on request. Disabled facilities are not the most suitable – but every effort will be made to help. **Parent and baby** – no facilities

While anyone privileged enough to visit Dalmore would leave immeasurably richer, the tour is at best for those who have visited distilleries elsewhere and can savour the richness of what is on offer. Prepare to spend time and to marvel at it all. You will treasure an experience as balanced as the malt. The aftertaste too will linger not just on the palate, but in the memory. In awarding the maximum seven stills we have had to throw in a condenser as well! Make an appointment now!

Overall rating

GLENMORANGIE

The home of one of the great malts does not disappoint. Stills are the highlight of a sound tour.

On the coast, half-a-mile (800m) north of Tain, Glenmorangie stands solid and proud. Built in warm sandstone, its original stillroom is now an outstanding visitor centre. The new Dutch barn-roofed stillroom blends in perfectly with a range of buildings extending from the reservoir at the top of this sloping site, to the warehouse with its flower beds at the bottom beside the railway line to Wick and Thurso. It is no surprise that Scotland's favourite malt whisky is distilled and matured here from barley grown in adjoining fields. It all feels right and comfortable.

Established 1843

Enquiries 01862 892477

Website www.glenmorangie.com

Opening hours All year, Mon-Fri, 9am-5pm; Jun-Aug, Sat, 10am-4pm; Sun, 12-4pm.

Getting there On the main A9 just north of Tain – no need to go into the town to get there, although it's a pleasant place to visit.

Parking/reception A little confusing – they seem to be a bit short of signs. Turn in from the A9, then left onto the old road, bear right, and the car park is on the left – a bit rough but with nice sea views. Disabled parking is straight on just before the shop on the left hand side. Reception is on the right in the former stillroom where a really friendly welcome awaits. There is a cornucopia of things to browse – a 130-year-old steam engine (Chrystals of Perth) an old green mill you can open and peer inside and superb

artistic woodcuts. This place is full of character – not the work of an 'off the peg' distillery interior decor guru.

Tour frequency Regularly from 10.30am on each half-hour. Winter tours at 10.30am, 11.30am, 2.30pm and 3.30pm.

Maximum group size 25

Cost £2.00. Redeemable in shop.

Group bookings Maximum 15 – pre-booking advisable.

Visual aids Video – good on the process, a bit of soft-sell on the product.

Foreign visitors Guides speak Italian, French and German. Leaflets in main European languages and Japanese.

Photography in distillery? Yes

Disabled access Restricted to exhibition area, warehouse, shop and refreshment room.

THE PRODUCT

Malt	Glenmorangie
Owner	Glenmorangie plc
Region	Highland (northern)
Ages	10 &18 years old and the wood-finish range

Water source Tarlogie Spring. The water is, most unusually, hard and rich in minerals.

Malting The last distillery to grow its own barley in the fields nearby. Lightly-peated at Glen Ord Maltings.

Bond 14 warehouses, mainly traditional earthen floors with barrels three high giving a cool stability to maturation with their thick stone and slate roofs. Some modern ones with eleven 'layers'.

Casks Ex-bourbon, used three times, with the last filling going for blending. 'Wood finish' malts are matured for 12 years in bourbon and two more in port, sherry or Madeira.

Bottling Broxburn, Lothian.

Experts' opinion The ten year old is light in colour, fresh, salty and nutty on the nose. Smooth, medium-dry with a subtle hint of peat. One to linger over and savour.

Our dram Whether due to the hard water, the sea air, or the tall stills, or all of these, a Glenmorangie is unmistakeable – delicate, exquisitely balanced, a hint of smokiness, and the lighter colour of the bourbon-only casks. No wonder it is in the top three sellers worldwide. We were also offered a dram of the port 'wood finish' – the overlay of port is not enough to mask the original, but sufficient to enhance it.

A good thorough tour – ordered, clear, lucid, with some humour. Pace was pleasurably unhurried. The warehouse, unusually, was the highlight. Glenmorangie even pick the trees, in the Ozarks, for their barrels before 'lending' them to bourbon distillers for four years. The groups tend to be large which can make it a little difficult to hear everything.

Special features The 9.5-tonne capacity mashtun and six stainless steel washbacks are best passed quickly – interesting for their part in the fermentation process, well-explained, but dull. Give me Scottish larch or Oregon pine any time. Would Glenmorangie be even better if fermented in wood – we think so! Reach the stillroom and all is forgiven. Modern but dignified it has a lofty Dutch barn wooden roof to accommodate the two rows of eight stills which, at 16ft 10in (5.1m) high, are among the loftiest in the land, although no match for Jura's. Originally gin stills (at a bargain price) these are unique (as tall as Glenfiddich's are small). They taper to the narrowest of necks and long small-bore lyne arms – only the lightest of spirit manages to pass into those lovely copper condensers. The spirit safe is lengthy and elegant – it has a lot of business to cope with. Like the stills it bears the name of McMillan of Prestonpans. Adjacent to it, a space-age console is set in a handsome wooden case. The warehouse with its aromas, vistas of rows of casks of all sizes, with port, oloroso sherry and Madeira as well as bourbon, is a treat to be shared with the angels.

Access Not easy – narrow stairs and passages and a lot of upping and downing.

Visual impact The stainless steel mashtun and washbacks are decidedly ungripping. By contrast the stills are so narrow and tall as to be genuinely spectacular (cooled by snow possibly!). The warehouse is superb too.

Range A full range of Glenmorangie whisky along with other company bottlings. Branded fleeces, rugby and polo shirts, shortbread, biscuits and mustards. It is also possible to buy your very own Glenmorangie driver and golf balls and even a jigsaw of local scenes unique to the distillery.

Style Pleasantly modern, all the colours of a Glenmorangie label.

Staff Tucked behind a big counter, but friendly and anxious to assist.

Catering There is a refreshment lounge close to the toilet area where coffee and cold drinks can be purchased from vending machines.

Toilets Good, modern, clean, facilities. Beautifully tiled and painted in Glenmorangie colours. Modern toilet facilities for the disabled.

An excellent tour of the home of one of the great malts, in a setting of some grandeur. The emphasis on the importance of wood is striking – effecting 60% of the flavour and character. Trees selected in the Ozark Mountains and casks from Spain, Portugal and Madeira. How odd to find such soulless steel washbacks! However you define it, though, the magic ingredient is still there, although the gin stills must by now be like the old wife's broom – original but for the head, the bristles and the handle. A top priority for beginners and aficionados alike. (Think 'orange' when you pronounce the name.)

Overall rating

GLEN ORD

Nice blend of tradition and modernity. Attractive visitor centre. Special tour with tastings, good value.

The first thing you see when you arrive in the vicinity is the tall modern factory-style maltings, but persevere because round the corner is a handsome distillery with twin pagodas and the dark stone of the warehouses offset nicely by the cream of the distillery buildings. The car park has lots of flowers and shrubs and some picnic tables. While less 'family-farm' than some, the appearance is pleasing and Muir of Ord is a couthy town in its own right.

Established 1838

Enquiries 01463 872004

Website www.glenord.com

Opening hours Mar-Oct, Mon-Fri, 9.30am-5pm; Jul-Sep, Sat, 9.30am-5pm; Sun, 12.30pm-5pm; Nov-Jan, restricted tours. Feb, 1pm-3.30pm. Call in advance.

Getting there About 18m/29km north of Inverness. Take the A832 road from Muir of Ord (the link to Contin and the A835 Kyle of Lochalsh road). In three quarters of a mile (1.2km) you will see the distillery on the junction of the A832 and the Altgowrie road. The distillery is on the right just beyond the towering Glen Ord Maltings .

Parking/reception Car park is on the right just before the distillery warehouses and reception. The first warehouse has been pleasantly adapted in 'Glen Ord' green with its cast-iron pillars trimmed in gold. There is a friendly welcome at the desk and a spacious

exhibition area in which to await your tour guide.

Tour frequency As required – every 10 minutes when busy.

Maximum group size 15

Cost £3.00. Redeemable in shop. Under-8s not allowed in distillery. Over-8s are free.

Group bookings By appointment with visitor centre.

Visual aids A video on the history and products is available while you wait for the tour. There is an exhibition of artefacts, and a display of cooperage as part of the tour.

Foreign visitors Guides speak Dutch, French and German. Leaflets in the main languages and Czech.

Photography in distillery? No

Disabled access Tour excellent for the disabled – access is good everywhere and assistance is unobtrusive – a real plus.

THE PRODUCT

Malt   Glen Ord

Owner   UDV

Region   Highland (northern)

Ages   12 & 23 year old 'Rare Malt'

Water source From two small lochs, nam Bonnach and nan Eun. Feeds the White Burn which flows over peat and granite.

Malting At Glen Ord Maltings right next door. 85% is grown locally and lightly peated. Malt for Talisker, Clynelish, Teaninich and Glenmorangie comes from here too.

Bond Five traditional warehouses on site – there is a view of one through glass from the

dram room – three rows high, but a bit distant and remote – no heady aromas!

Casks Ex-bourbon and sherry (used twice).

Bottling At Leven in Fife.

Experts' opinion Amber in colour, sweet, malty, with a light sherry note (some find this obtrusive) rich and fresh with a dry peppery finish – 'perilously drinkable'.

Our dram A twelve year old – we shouldn't have had to ask for water! A nice fresh nose, slightly sweet and malty, with just a soupçon of peat. Pleasant finish – easy to drink but not overwhelmingly characterful. Changes in name and nature (it used to be called Glenordie) perhaps account to some extent for that.

The tour starts with a good introduction to malting, fermenting and distilling, and some excellent Scottish history. Humour and expertise are revealed, and questions fielded competently. The pace can be a little hasty – but it is better than the normal tourist experience.

Special features An impressive cast-iron mashtun, painted dark green and with a nicely proportioned copper canopy. It has a 12.5-tonne grist capacity. Close by is the wort cooler – all steel plates and pipes, and a few yards away eight dark brown Oregon-pine washbacks with broad green hoops – they are almost 40 years old and settling in well. Their true height can be appreciated as the mesh on the floor is broad and revealing. The stillroom is modern – rather like Caol Ila's but without the view. Visitors walk under the lyne arms between splendidly lacquered stills and their condensers. All in a row and appearing to be of similar size, the six stills were built by Abercrombie of Alloa. It makes an impressive array – they are of graceful single-onion shape and taper away elegantly. The spirit safe is long and well-proportioned with the brass set off by two gleaming copper urns above (for the stillman's 'cuppa' perhaps?). Only the absence of milling and a real warehouse experience detracts from the whole.

Access Excellent – very few steps and nothing too steep. Ramps at some points.

Visual impact Externally pretty in cream roughcast and nice pagodas. Internally smart and a spicy mix of modern and traditional.

SHOP

Range Glen Ord and Classic Malts range, glasses, prints, books and a limited range of 'Glen Ord green' apparel.

Style Twinned with reception – gold tops to the pillars, nice spot, brightly lit with well-laid-out displays. A transformation of a gloomy warehouse but with the atmosphere preserved.

Staff Friendly and helpful.

Catering None. Hotels and cafés in Muir of Ord nearby. Excellent fish and chips in Beauly.

Toilets Green with wood trim – resplendent and immaculate. Really well laid out loos for the disabled. **Parent and baby** – no facilities, but books and toys in the dram room and orange juice available as well.

SUMMARY

Not the prettiest of distilleries but not at all bad. Tradition and modernity are nicely blended on one level for the visitor and the tour is competently handled. A good beginner's tour. For the cognoscenti there is a £10 de-luxe tour which is combined with tastings of the Classic Malts and others, conducted by the estimable and knowledgeable Catherine Gray. Highly recommended.

Overall rating

HIGHLAND PARK

Superb welcome with coffee and short-bread then an all-embracing tour including floor maltings. A fine traditional distillery. Worth the pilgrimage to Orkney on its own.

On high ground behind Kirkwall, with splendid seaviews to Shapinsay and beyond, the distillery looks its age. It is not spectacularly beautiful – there are too many pipes and appurtenances for that. But the overall grouping and the stone of the buildings – dark-grey, almost black – is satisfying and the courtyard bounded by the mash and tun rooms, the shop and coffee room is pleasant and well-proportioned. Glimpses of the twin pagodas can be had from here. Stay at the quaint Ferry Inn at Stromness and watch the boats come in and go out – remember to order the lobster thermidor (in advance) for dinner – wonderful.

Established 1798

Enquiries 01856 874619

Website www.highland.co.uk

Opening hours Apr-Oct, Mon-Fri, 10am-5pm; Jul-Sep; Sat-Sun, 12-5pm, Nov-Mar: tour is at 2pm only. Shop open 1pm-5pm, Mon-Fri.

Getting there From Stromness on the A964 turn right on outskirts of Kirkwall at an Esso garage into Pickquoy Road, then at T-junction turn right and after a bit join the A961 for South Ronaldsay. The distillery is on the left.

Parking/reception Parking is on the right opposite distillery entrance. As you enter the courtyard bear right up the stairs into the coffee shop where Elsie will give you the warmest of Orkney welcomes. There is a video loop to watch and beautifully painted sketches which illustrate the steps in the distilling process. Soon your tour guide will be there to greet you and take you off to the joys of the malting floor.

Tour frequency Every half hour.

Maximum group size 15

Cost £3.00.

Group bookings Book in advance to avoid disappointment. Cruise ship parties welcomed.

Visual aids While downing your dram post-tour, there is an excellent 10-minute video – visually beautiful and with an excellent summary of Orkney history.

Foreign visitors Audio-visual in English, French, German, Italian. Guides speak Norwegian, French and German and there are excellent leaflets in these and Japanese.

Photography in distillery? No

Disabled access Staff pride themselves in tours for the disabled – maltings, kilns, mash and tun rooms (a bit limited) stillroom and warehouses are all accessible. Coffee shop is not on but staff will bring tea and buns to you in the shop area. Special help for deaf visitors – 'signing' possible by arrangement.

THE PRODUCT

Malt Highland Park

Owner Highland Distillers

Region Island

Ages 12, 18, & 25 years old. 21-year-old Bicentennial and limited editions. 12-year-old cask strength.

Water source Cattie Maggie's spring.

Malting 80% malted at Tamdhu and the rest on the distillery floors. 18 hours of peat-fired drying in the kilns followed by 30 hours with coke results in fairly heavily peated malt. Peat from Hobbister on Scapa Flow is shallow-cut so that the heather and salt from the sea-spray add to the taste.

Bond 26 warehouses on site or nearby ranging from traditional to modern.

Casks Ex-bourbon and sherry.

Bottling Drumchapel, Glasgow.

Experts' opinion Full of character, smoky, heather-honeyish, lingering long and with a big satisfying finish.

Our dram The 12 year old is distinctive and delicious – relatively dark in colour, with the heather and peat prominent and a lovely after-taste – a real 'anytime' dram. The 18 and 25 year olds are smoother, mellower, but maybe with a little less character. If you can get it, the Bicentennial 21 is the tops – as full of character as the 12, as smooth as the 25, but with an extra peaty magic (we mean it).

An excellent tour with a competent, friendly guide, and with the great bonus of visiting the malting floors, where everything is clearly explained. Distillery staff chip in with little gems as you pass, and questions are welcomed. The pace is not leisurely, but then there is so much to see. Microphones and speakers in the mashhouse and stillroom make it easy to hear above the clamour. A good tour – a pity you can't get close to the aromas of the washbacks, but staff are working on that.

Special features Where to start! The malting floors are wonderful – on the ground level, with two floors set in an unusual 'Y' shape, with the steeps above. The chariots for spreading and the wooden spades for turning, together with the modern mechanical turners, can all be seen in use. Then on to the two kilns – the 'old' one over 100 years old, the 'new' one which is a mere 80. To see and smell the peat – with its high heather content, and to 'feel' the smoke drying the grain above – is evocative in the extreme, so rarely experienced nowadays. Then to a combined mash and tun room. Visitors look down on the steel mashtun – a fair size and able to gobble 9.5 tonnes of grist. It has a rather graceful, shiny, steel canopy to admire. The view of the 12 washbacks is more distant – but they look old – natural Oregon pine in colour, with old-fashioned circular-section red hoops. The mash house and tun room are in the former stillroom (look out there for the old furnace arches now filled in with stone) and it is a short walk from there to the 'new' stillroom, which looks pretty old. Inside are four stills – two slightly larger wash stills (with blue condensers outside) and two spirit stills with copper condensers. Hard-working rather than lacquer-manicured, all four are sturdy, big and purposeful. Slightly tapering to the neck, they have medium-bore lyne arms – just right somehow for these northern climes and the robust character of the malt they produce. The spirit safe in splendid brass is elegant – typical of the work of Archibald McMillan of Edinburgh. If you are lucky the stillman will 'dip' the spirit receiver and let you sniff the raw spirit. The warehouse is really old, gloomy, and has the thickest black mould in the business. The viewing gallery gives a good view and vents above the glass allow the angels' share to permeate through – delicious! The audio-visual (often one of the distillery cats joins you here for a cuddle) ends the tour and lets you see the fermentation in the washbacks, even if you can't smell it! These same washbacks, would you believe, were filled with hot water during the last war to allow some of the 60,000 servicemen on Orkney to bathe!

Access Access is good, but as the distillery is old, you have to mind your head and your footing but it adds to the traditional feel of the place.

Visual impact Not a showpiece, but none the worse for that – 'period' traditional feel, with peat smells and sturdy working stills.

Range Whisky, glasses, jugs, flasks, decanters, watches, teddy bears, books, pictures, pens, cheese, herring, goodie hampers and much more.

Style Adapted from a former stable, attractively warm, nicely lit, well-laid-out displays.

Staff Orkney gems every one. The pace is Orkney but the service is superb, running even to a gift service for distant relatives (perhaps a keyring) and good friends (at least a bottle of the 25 year old).

Catering Coffee shop with tea, coffee, soft drinks, biscuits, shortbread and cake. Orkney Ice Cream too.

Toilets Beside the shop and better than at home! Fresh flowers even. Excellent loo for the disabled beside the shop – unfortunately in the ladies' toilets. **Parent and baby** – no facilities. Puzzles and quizzes are provided for young ones who might find the tour boring.

A superb welcome, (even from the mouser cat), a really all-embracing tour of a fine old working distillery, a dram of one of the best malts, an excellent video, a coffee and shortbread with Elsie to start or finish with – what more can you ask for? Combine your visit with Orkney's many delights: archaeology is fun at Skara Brae with more recent history at the Italian Chapel. Here, nature is at its unpolluted best: so much of Orkney is unspoiled and the sun shines incessantly (I made that bit up)!

Overall rating

Unromantic working distillery but the stills and lyne arms are a conversation stopper.

In a broad backstreet amidst low tenemental houses, there are few clues to its identify – no pagodas, simply warehouses and an old factory building. There is a wrought-iron gate, and the office is to the right – smart with a lovely brass plate and a 'drifter' window. What you see is what you get – workmanlike, but hardly worth getting the camera out for. The release of Old Pulteney malt by the owners a few years ago was widely welcomed as it had always been a fairly rare dram to track down. Clever marketing of the malt with strong associations made to the fishing trade in the North of Scotland and excellent presentation and packaging have also helped the whisky gain a distinctive foothold in the marketplace.

Established 1826

Enquiries 01955 602371

Website www.inverhouse.com

Opening hours Apr-Dec, Mon-Fri, 10am-3pm; Jan-Mar, Mon-Fri, restricted hours. All visits by appointment. Can be closed to tours in the summer. Call in advance to confirm.

Getting there There is no easy way! Entering Wick on the A99 from the south look out for Northcote Street on the right, then go left into Macrae Street, then immediately right into Rutherford Street. From the centre of Wick follow the south side of the harbour and turn up the hill at the end.

Parking/reception Outside in the street is best as the courtyard is restricted. Enter from the street, pay in the shop and move through to the visitor centre, along a passage reminiscent of a sailing ship's bridge complete with

wheel. The shop has stained glass 'herring drifter' windows, to underline the distillery's origins – supplying a spirit to keep the fisher folk happy. A quiet, friendly welcome and a chance to admire the central wall hangings and feel the flagged floors beneath your feet.

Tour frequency At 11am and 2pm.

Maximum group size 10

Cost £2.50. Redeemable in shop.

Group bookings By appointment only.

Visual aids Visitor centre displays illustrate the process. Good cooperage display as well.

Foreign visitors No facilities.

Photography in distillery? Yes

Disabled access Tour unsuitable for the less then spry apart from the stillhouse and the visitor centre.

THE PRODUCT

Malt Old Pulteney

Owner Inver House Distillers Ltd

Region Highland (northern)

Ages 12 & 15 years old

Water source Loch Hempriggs

Malting Unpeated. Prisma variety, malted at Kirkcaldy in Fife.

Bond Two large warehouses on site.

Casks Ex-bourbon and sherry.

Bottling At Inver House Distillers, Airdrie, Lanarkshire.

Experts' opinion Well-matured at 12 years, delicate light aroma, merest touch of the island malts, fresh with a smoky finish. A welcome return of a good pre-dinner dram – every sip a voyage of discovery.

Our dram Taken in the visitor centre – fairly pale, medium-dry, with a North-east touch of the sea – the warehouse sojourn perhaps or that adventurous voyage down and round the lyne arms? Clean fresh, slightly sweet finish.

A quiet standard tour of a working distillery which makes few concessions to glamour or grandeur. Most of what visitors need to see is here and there are good worm's eye views of the stills. The pace is congenial and small groups enable everyone to see and hear.

Special features Your visit starts with the fine maroon Porteous mill. The mashtun is an old cast-iron item made by Newmills Engineering of Elgin, and thought to have come from Oban. At one time open-topped, it now has a smart, shiny, stainless steel canopy and a step up to peer in – its lauter arm is unusually sturdy. En route to the washbacks the tour takes visitors past a 'period' heat exchanger, half car radiator, half as if from an old farm creamery. The five washbacks are unique in appearance – the outer skin is steel, painted silver, and the interior is stainless steel. The tops are white steel with small utilitarian wooden hatches – interesting yes, elegant decidedly not! There is a wooden roof to the tun room and the broad mesh floor lets you see the full depth of the washbacks. The two stills make up for it all – fairly stubby with a big double-onion, and after a broad swan neck they spout unique lyne arms which curl down and round, for all the world like a copper tuba, to join condensers half their height, but twice the circumference of more usual items. The spirit safe is tucked away in a nook and is small with lovely copper pipes above and a small copper urn behind (for the stillman's cuppa again?). It bears no maker's plaque but a brass plate proudly proclaims 'Pulteney Distillery' with a star above.

Access Fairly difficult with steep stairs and narrow passageways.

Visual impact Industrial rather than traditional. The lyne arms don't half catch the eye.

Range Old Pulteney, Catto's blend, glasses, fudge, liqueurs, teeshirts, sweatshirts and fleeces, and a Pulteney putter in fine brass. Where is the consoling flask in the handle for missed putts?

Style Nautical flavour with fine pine floors and partitions, rope fiddles on the tables and those lovely windows. The owners financed the restoration of the drifter *Isabella Fortuna*.

Staff Quiet, helpful and friendly tour guides.

Catering None – but Wick boasts a fine range of eating places. The fish and chips take some beating – to our certain knowledge.

Toilets Upstairs – clean and modern. No toilets for the disabled. **Parent and baby** – no facilities.

Wick is one of those places you seldom get to by design, and Pulteney is not so attractive that a special trip should be contemplated by the less than committed. If you happen to be in the area, fairly fit and curious, then a good average tour of a working distillery is on offer, which furnishes a sound, if unromantic introduction to the subject. For the serious anorak the lyne arms alone make the trip worthwhile.

Overall rating

TOMATIN

Big, but not beautiful with all the elegance of a gasworks. Tours laboured and views restricted. Your romantic illusions of distilleries will certainly be shattered!

At 1,028ft/313m above sea level, this is the second-highest distillery in Scotland. Situated close to good water supplies. It looks its best from the main Inverness railway line as Tomatin occupies a pleasant site with some handsome distillery houses close by. Sadly all the older buildings have disappeared – there are no pagodas or maltings to be seen, and while its size can be appreciated, it is not a place to linger, far less to picnic. In Gaelic Tomatin means 'hill of the juniper berries' – if only it still was. Perhaps Scottish gin was once distilled here!

Established 1897

Enquiries 01808 511444

Website None

Opening hours Easter-end Oct, Mon-Fri, 9am-4.30pm; May-Sept, Sat, 9.30am-12.30pm.

Getting there On the A9 Perth to Inverness trunk road, 16 miles (25km) south of Inverness. Distillery is signposted.

Parking/reception Follow signs and then arrows on road to car park – watch the pillars. Disabled parking is at the visitor centre. Follow signs to visitor centre. You are invited to join the tour or simply to watch a very good video (or both). There are good dia-grams to study, an old spirit safe working away – sadly with only water flowing through it – and display cases to browse.

Tour frequency As required.

Maximum group size 15

Cost Free.

Group bookings Prior notice is required for large parties.

Visual aids Excellent video.

Foreign visitors Leaflets in French, German and Italian.

Photography in distillery? No

Disabled access Access to visitor centre, stillhouse and warehouse only.

THE PRODUCT

Malt Tomatin

Owner Tomatin Distillery Co

Region Highland (northern)

Ages 10 & 19 year old (cask-strength)

Water source Allt-na-Frithe – or 'Free Burn' – a tributary of the River Findhorn.

Malting Barley is malted at Moray Firth Maltings at Inverness and is lightly peated.

Bond There are 16 warehouses on site containing 12 million gallons (54.5 million litres) of spirit. One cooper is still employed on site. The warehouse we visited has excellent displays of barrels and (belatedly!) malt samples. There is even a lifelike exciseman sitting in his office.

Casks Ex-bourbon and sherry.

Bottling Blending, uniquely, is on site including the celebrated Antiquary. Bottling is carried out by Wm Muir & Co at Leith. Gordon and MacPhail bottle some expressions of Tomatin in Elgin.

Experts' opinion Pale amber in colour. Hint of oak and sweetness on the nose. Medium-sweet, lightly smoky, well-rounded with a gentle finish – definitely a pre-dinner dram.

Our dram We had a laboured 'sell' mainly of the blends before sampling the 10-year-old malt. It is hard to define, perhaps lacking in outright character, but it is light, malty and smooth. Our view is that it is at its best in the superb 12-year-old Antiquary blend.

A below average tour by guides full of charm, but seemingly lacking in training and confidence. Difficult to follow and to hear. Answers to straightforward questions tended to be vague and even inaccurate. The pace is appropriate but the marshalling is a bit mechanistic with limited views, particularly of the stills and there was some confusion about washbacks and mashtuns.

Special features By 1974 this was Scotland's largest malt whisky distillery with a potential capacity of 5 million proof gallons (22.7 million litres) per annum. From two stills in 1956, it has grown to 23. Unfortunately this has been at the price of turning it into a rather unsightly factory – all pipes and gantries, with Heath-Robinson pipework (none of it in copper) and to say it is functional is putting the best possible gloss on it. If you have any illusions about the romance of distilling, prepare to shed them here. There are two Porteous mills – the older one made in Leeds, the newer in Hull. Then on to two lauter mashtuns one above the other on separate floors. The upper one is probably the one in use and is a modern job by Balfour of Leven – stainless steel, graceless, redeemed by a nicely shaped canopy. In a gloomy hall there are 12 stainless steel washbacks which no doubt are efficient (next door are six cast-iron disused ones – much nicer with yellow exteriors and smart black covers). The stillhouse is huge with 12 wash stills on one side and 11 spirit stills on the other, all with stubby external condensers. As far as one can see, they are onion-shaped with a bulge ('belted in' with brass hoops). They are of medium size, quite narrow at the top, with straight lyne arms. There are no less than seven spirit safes in two banks, made by Grant of Dufftown – sadly situated on top of ugly grey racking. All in all, not a very pretty sight. Fortunately the warehouse has traditional earthen floors and racking.

Access Limited – mashtuns and washbacks can be left out (on Saturdays they always are!) and stills can only be seen by peering up through a mass of pipes and mesh-flooring.

Visual impact Unloved – heavily industrial, with no aesthetic appeal at all – even the 23 stills fail to excite (they are not all in use at one time but what a pity you can't see any of them clearly).

Range Whisky – malt and blends – Athol Brose and Heather Cream, fudge, honey, glasses and decanters.

Style Low-roofed modern building with display case and counter service.

Staff Friendly but stressed – hard to be enthusiastic about their surroundings.

Catering None – and there is nothing nearby.

First-time fellow visitors from abroad found Tomatin interesting but deeply disappointing when set against their preconceptions of a Scottish distillery. Let's face it, it's not very bonny and proves conclusively that size isn't everything. With a mediocre tour experience, it has, in all honesty, not got a lot going for it when compared with so many outstanding experiences available elsewhere. Best admired from the sleeper en route to Inverness!

Overall rating

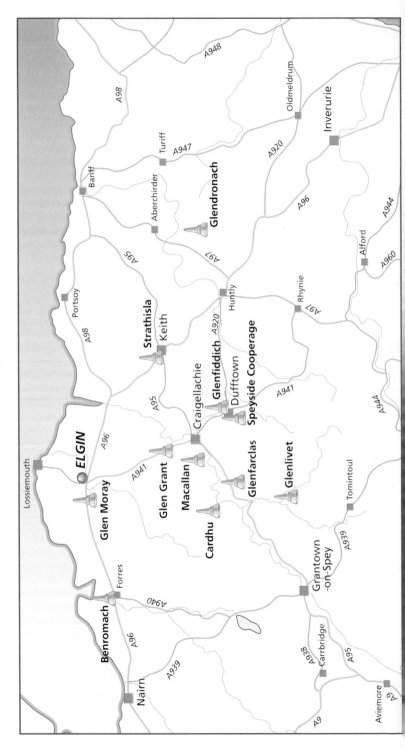

Speyside

Try to visit Speyside in May when the colours are vivid, the gorse and broom at their most yellow, and when the weather can be at its best (except when the haar comes in from the Moray Firth). October colours have their attractions too. Speyside is the epicentre of malt whisky production, with nine distilleries to choose from, as well as the not-to-be-missed Speyside Cooperage at Craigellachie. There is the official Scotch Whisky Trail to follow but it's really a case of choosing what is most convenient for you. Unless you feel up to all ten facilities, read the entries which follow carefully. Some are for connoisseurs, some for casual visitors, and some are simply unmissable. Others, quite frankly, are a bit dull.

Elgin is as good a centre as any. We can recommend Mansfield House (01343 540883) – it's always worth going where the locals go! Another base is Craigellachie (close to the shrine of Macallan) where the Craigellachie Hotel (01340 881204) has classic Speyside ambience and a fine selection of malts. A passable snack, or elevenses, can be had while visiting the Speyside Cooperage. For caravanners, the most delightful site is nearby at the Camping and Caravanning Club site on the B9102. It lies midway between Macallan and Cardhu and is beautiful, friendly and smack in the middle of the action. Although a little bit away, bikers will enjoy the views and the welcome at Alton Burn in Nairn (01667 452051). Speyside, with well-maintained and peaceful roads with the perfect ratio of curves to vistas, offers everything a touring biker could wish for.

Visitors to Speyside should not neglect the coastline of the Moray Firth, which boasts a fine mix of beaches and picturesque fishing villages. Our personal favourites are Hopeman and Portsoy. For those of a sporting disposition, the most challenging of many fine golf courses in the area is at Nairn (watch out for the whin bushes). For the salmon angler there is an embarrassment of riches – at a price. Those looking for brown trout rather than salmon will find that there is excellent sport to be had in the Huntly area, and around Alford on the River Don. If bites are hard to come by, there is often a lesson to be had from the ospreys on the excellently managed Castle Forbes beats.

BENROMACH

CARDHU

GLENDRONACH

GLENFARCLAS

GLENFIDDICH

GLEN GRANT

GLENLIVET

GLEN MORAY

MACALLAN

STRATHISLA

SPEYSIDE COOPERAGE

BENROMACH

Compact, attractive and modern. A good first tour with enough for the aficionado too.

Opened in 1898, closed in 1983, and reborn in 1998, Benromach is a delight to the eye – glistening, neat, white buildings, lovely old maltings (sadly disused) and that giant red chimney. There are gardens and picnic tables – a lovely spot to savour and conveniently close to the charms of Forres. The resurrection of this distillery by the independent bottlers and whisky merchants, Gordon & MacPhail of Elgin, is to be admired. Formerly a mothballed asset of United Distillers & Vintners, it is good to see enthusiastic independent companies like G&M moving into this sector of the whisky trade.

Established 1998

Enquiries 01309 675968

Website www.benromach.com

Opening hours Oct-Mar, Mon-Fri, 10am-4pm; Apr-Sep, Mon-Sat, 9.30am-5pm; Jun-Aug, Sun, 12-4pm.

Getting there 500yds/460m on the north side of the Forres bypass on the main A96 Aberdeen to Inverness road. Turn off at the signpost for Waterford.

Parking/reception Ample parking straight ahead as you enter. Disabled places are handily positioned. The centre opened with the distillery in 1998 and is a separate, spacious building. The welcome here is more professional than warm and a bit distant until the tour begins when things get better.

Tour frequency 20 mins.

Maximum group size 12

Cost £2.50. Redeemable in shop. Under-18s are free.

Group bookings If your group is 12 and over, telephone in advance.

Visual aids Small boards at key locations but they unfortunately are a bit difficult to read unless you have a magnifying glass in your sporran. Video for the disabled.

Foreign visitors Guide speaks French, German and Spanish.

Photography in distillery? No

Disabled access To visitor centre only.

THE PRODUCT

Malt Benromach

Owner Gordon & MacPhail

Region Speyside

Ages 15 & 18 years old (cask strength)

Water source Chapelton Springs, two miles (3.2km) away in the Ronach Hills

Malting Malted barley comes from various sources. Unusually for a Speyside, while mainly lightly peated, some of the barley used is heavily peated..

Bond Cask filling on view – from a lovely pine spirit vat. Warehouse on site, traditional and worth seeing.

Casks Ex-bourbon and sherry

Bottling Gordon & MacPhail, Elgin – where else!

Experts' opinion A pleasant amber colour, a touch of apple and peatiness, long gentle smoky fresh, ending in a pronounced maltiness. An excellent pre-dinner dram. It will be 2010 before the new post-1998 Benromach is bottled, so it's just as well there are reserves of the 15 year old available.

Our dram A generous one! More body and oiliness on the palate then most Speysides – an extra hint of peat – very pleasant indeed.

With the mashtun, washbacks and stills virtually all in one room, it is easy to take in the whole process without too much gadding about. The tour is competently handled and the steps are easy to follow. Technical questions could catch the guide out, but working staff were able to give most of the answers. The pace is right, the route well thought out and, as a result, the visitor can see more detail than in some larger distilleries.

Special features New, small and perfectly formed. First a tiny mill (Boby of Bury St. Edmunds) then a dinky mashtun of insulated steel, with a really handsome copper top. Close by are five new washbacks made of Scottish larch, with nice red hoops. How pleasant that the owners were not tempted, as others have been, by the claimed convenience of stainless steel. Across from the washbacks are the wash and spirit stills of double-onion shape and straight necks in lacquered copper. The condensers are outside, close to the spectacular and totally free-standing 100ft/20m red-brick chimney. The brass spirit safe (Abercrombie of Alloa, 1980) is small and elegant. Down below the stillroom, most unusually, is a pristine, tiled hall where you can see the bottom of the stills where the heat is directly applied – the whole thing is 'guid gear in sma' bulk' – a year's output would take but a week for one of the big boys!

Access The smallest distillery on Speyside, but access is good. An easy tour on the body.

Visual impact New, small, compact – most attractive, outside and in. Like the Isle of Arran Distillery at Lochranza, designed with visitors in mind.

SHOP

Range Whiskies – Benromach and Gordon & MacPhail bottlings, along with glasses, branded woollens, marmalade and shortbread. A full range of Gordon & MacPhail's malt bottlings can be seen at the shop in South Street, Elgin, which doubles as a cracking delicatessen.

Style Elegant glass display cases in the visitor centre – hands off!

Staff Your guide will attend to your needs.

Catering None on site – Forres has much to offer.

Toilets Exemplary, well-maintained, spotless. Excellent loo for the disabled. **Parent and baby** – no facilities provided.

SUMMARY

Compact, modern, attractive. The Benromach tour is an easy one, not too long, and yet you see all you need to see to understand the process. Ideal for a first or casual visit, but different enough to titillate and stimulate the aficionado. The glimpse beneath the stills and the atmospheric exterior of the traditional warehouse are arresting.

Overall rating

CARDHU

Pretty distillery in attractive setting.
Good tour – bring a picnic!

The site is high in the hills with stunning Speyside views from the windows and the gardens complete with picnic tables. The buildings provide a nice contrast of cream walls and stone, and the former maltings look splendid with a brand-new pagoda on top – sadly ornamental nowadays. This is a wonderful place to be, particularly if you are lucky enough to be there on a sunny summer day.

Established 1824

Enquiries 01340 872552

Website None

Opening hours Jan/Feb, Mon-Fri, 11am-3pm; Mar-Jun, Mon-Fri, 10am-4.30pm; Jul-Sep, Mon-Fri, 10am-6pm; Sat, 10am-4.30pm; Sun, 11am-4pm; Oct, Mon-Fri, 10am-4.30pm; Nov/Dec, Mon-Fri, 11am-3pm.

Getting there On the B9102 Grantown to Craigellachie road, in Knockando, a village seven miles (11.2km) from Craigellachie.

Parking/reception Parking is to the right of the distillery. Disabled parking is at the visitor centre, recently refurbished with a friendly welcome and invitation to join the next tour. You return to reception at the end of the tour having savoured your dram in the warehouse – a good idea.

Tour frequency 10-15 mins as required. Last tour one hour before closing.

Maximum group size 12

Cost £3.00. Redeemable in shop.

Group bookings Not suitable for coach tours. Smaller groups by arrangement.

Visual aids Excellent model of a working maltings. Video for the disabled.

Foreign visitors Process explained in reception. Handboards at key points in French, German, Italian, and Spanish.

Photography in distillery? Yes

Disabled access To visitor centre only but tour can be joined in the warehouse for a dram. A nice touch!

THE PRODUCT

Malt Cardhu

Owner UDV

Region Speyside

Ages 12 & 18 years old

Water source Marrich Hill Spring

Malting Carried out at Burghead.

Bond There is a viewing gallery in the bonded warehouse.

Casks Ex-bourbon only – used up to five times rather than the more normal two or three.

Bottling In Kilmarnock where two thirds of Cardhu goes for blending to make that famous blend – Johnnie Walker – 'born 1820 and still going strong'.

Experts' opinion Clean and delicately balanced – a bouquet of ripe pears and carnations – hints of sandalwood and Parma violets (whatever they are!).

Our dram Unusually you take your ample dram in the viewing area of the warehouse, savouring it as the guide explains the cask sizes. It is a good way to do it, especially as Cardhu is a smooth, mellow, whisky with a hint of apple and a pleasing aftertaste.

Good clear concise 'standard' tour covering all the ground thoroughly; a nice mix of history and distilling. The tour is well-organised, the distillery bright and spacious, enabling everyone to see, hear and ask questions. The pace is spot-on for relaxed enjoyment.

Special features First the Porteous mill and the model of a maltings at work, then the mashtun made of stainless steel resplendent with copper canopy. On to to eight splendid washbacks of Scottish larch – the tour guide leads you downstairs passing close beside them, giving you an opportunity to appreciate their great size. The stillroom has three large wash stills and three smaller spirit stills, all with long, straight necks (these being the key to the flavour of Cardhu) and a new copper spirit safe installed in 1999. Cardhu (Gaelic for 'black rock') is bottled in a distinctive pinched bottle and topped with a traditional beech-capped cork stopper.

Access Good, safe and comprehensive – a bit of a climb to the mash room.

Visual impact Clean and immaculate – nice blend of craft and science, space-age with a human face.

SHOP

Range Good range of UDV malts, glasses, umbrellas etc.

Style In reception area – cosy, attractive, in cream and light wood.

Staff Tour guides serve you and are really helpful – particularly to disabled visitors

Catering None. Bring a flask and sit in the garden area – perhaps not in January!

Toilets Ladies and disabled loo in reception area are spotless and sweet smelling although not immediately visible as there are no signs – some embarassment potential here perhaps. Excellent loo for the disabled. **Parent and baby** – in ladies area.

SUMMARY

This is one of the better experiences for the visitor, enhanced by beautiful surroundings. A nice balance between those tours which make no concessions to visitor needs, and the luxury ones whose cosettings can distract one from the purpose of the visit. If this is to be your only visit to a distillery, you will have chosen well. If you visit lots of them, this will assuredly add to the sum total of your knowledge.

Overall rating

GLENDRONACH

Honest, down-to-earth experience in mothballed distillery. Comprehensive tour with pawky humour content!

Comfortably set in Glendronach, 'the valley of the brambles' beside the river Dronach, the distillery is of traditional grey stone, apart from the stillroom with its glass walls. It is pleasing rather than arresting with warehouses, cottages, maltings and The Glen House, some 200 years old, grouped into a little village. It looks the way distilleries should look.

Established 1826

Enquiries 01466 730202

Website None

Opening hours All year, Mon-Fri, two tours per day.

Getting there On the A97 turn on to the B9001 six miles (10km) north of Huntly. After three miles (5km) turn right on to the B9024. The distillery is in 100yds/90m on the left.

Parking/reception Follow road into distillery centre, cars on left, coaches on right. Ignore the 'Reception' sign you see from the car park! From the car park the visitor centre is on the left of the lane to the left. The welcome is a mite subdued, and the reception area a little gloomy and spartan with tiled floors and some hard seats. However, as soon as Jean MacIrvine appears it gets better and better – you get your dram straight away (even at 10am) as you watch an excel-

lent video, and then you're off. Glendronach has been mothballed since 1997 and is due to re-open in 2001. This gives a slightly museum-like feel to the tour, but you see much more than elsewhere.

Tour frequency 10am and 2pm.

Maximum group size 20

Cost No charge.

Group bookings Will take groups or coaches outside tour hours by prior arrangement only.

Visual aids The video is colourful and informative. Models and artefacts illustrate how malting is carried out and there are good illustrations dotted about elsewere.

Foreign visitors Some German spoken.

Photography in distillery? Yes

Disabled access Limited to visitor centre. Malting floor and kiln can be viewed.

THE PRODUCT

Malt   Glendronach

Owner   Allied Distillers

Region   Speyside

Age   15 years old

Water source Spring water from the hills of the Dronach Valley.

Malting Distillery malting floors and kilns can be accessed and viewed.

Bond Viewing window in visitor centre.

Casks Ex-sherry only – used three times – samples can be viewed. Less 'marrying' is required with ex-sherry casks.

Bottling At Dumbarton.

Experts' opinion Smooth aroma, balanced, with smoky overtones and a long, dark, finish – good after-dinner dram and deservedly popular.

Our dram Dark in colour, needs a splash of water, fragrant toffee nose, a hint of peat, a trace of sherry – we liked it, but perhaps it's better after dinner than breakfast!

An excellent and comprehensive tour at a nice pace with pawky humour and human touches. By the end you know all you need to and you will have enjoyed the informality of the approach. Connoisseurs of Buchan humour will treasure the asides. There is a fair bit of dodging and ducking involved and some steep stairs, but it is well-controlled and everyone can see and hear.

Special features The mashtun looks like it was made from bits of the Forth Rail Bridge – all cast iron, bolts and flanges. It has a graceful copper top and the agitator is an old-fashioned horizontal arm on cogwheels – nice! Nine washbacks of Oregon pine – then on to a modern stillroom (1967) which, like those at Caol Ila, Aberfeldy and Clynelish, is a bit incongruous with large picture windows. The four elegant, lacquered, copper stills with curved necks and of double-onion shape are still coal-fired (ask Jean about the 'rummagers'). Two brass spirit safes gleam as you pass by. Keeping the best till last, Glendronach (until 1997 at least) did its own malting and this is one of only a handful of places where you can still see and smell the malting floors, the furnaces, and even peer up inside a pagoda kiln. You then follow the malt through milling (a 68-year-old Boby made in Bury St Edmunds) and into the mashtun as you climb the 19th-century alleyway steel stairs – just grand!

Access Need for care in the older parts – after the mashtun it's fairly easy with plenty to see.

Visual impact The maltings area is stunningly old-fashioned and atmospheric. The stillroom is splendid.

Range Glendronach and William Teacher's blends, Scapa malt from Orkney, marmalade, coasters, keyrings, pens, glasses, ashtrays, jugs and umbrellas.

Style Small, over-the-counter job. No concessions to fashion stylists, more like your local corner shop.

Staff Quiet but helpful.

Catering None.

Toilets Functional and clean. No disabled loo. **Parent and baby** – no facilities

There is nothing glossy about the experience and little money has been spent on glamour, but who can complain when there is no charge. You get an honest down-to-earth experience with more to see, especially the maltings, than in many a glitzier distillery. Recommended for beginners and aficionados alike – let's hope the lum reeks once more in 2001, but don't bet on it.

Overall rating

GLENFARCLAS

Quality tour. Lots to see. A graceful visitor centre with friendly staff, lovely panelling from a Canadian Pacific liner and great views of Ben Rinnes. Largest pot stills on Speyside.

The buildings are rather factory-like grouped round a courtyard and containing the farm where it all started. From a cream painted interior, metal framed windows allow splendid views of Ben Rinnes and the Spey Valley. Plenty of grass and trees to stroll and relax in. This distillery can honestly claim to be truly independent as it has been in the care of the Grant family over five generations since 1865.

Established 1836

Enquiries 01807 500209

Website www.glenfarclas.co.uk

Opening hours Oct-Mar, Mon-Fri, 10am-4pm; Apr-Sep, Mon-Fri, 10am-5pm; Jun-Sep, Sat, 10am-5pm.

Getting there On the A95, five miles (8km) west of Aberlour, turn left onto a short stretch of straight, narrow road and you are there.

Parking/reception At the front of the facility – turn left at the sign. Friendly greeting at attractive free-standing visitor centre dating from 1973 and recently splendidly refurbished, featuring a rather elegant copper still and, by contrast, a home-made 1830's version from a farm. The pagoda of the now disused maltings enhances the roofline. While away the time before your tour begins in the reception room which boasts oak panelling from the 1913

Canadian Pacific liner *Empress of Australia*. Astute chairman George Grant bought the decor in Rosyth in 1973. With its arched, Italian, plaster ceiling – a replica of the ship's smoking room ceiling – and views of Ben Rinnes, there is a quaint but pleasant illusion of cruising on dry land.

Tour frequency Every 15 mins.

Maximum group size 14

Cost £3.50. Redeemable in shop.

Group bookings By appointment – group rates are available.

Visual aids Some illustrations in visitor centre, malt and grist samples.

Foreign visitors There is no specific provision – your English has to be up to it or your bus-driver has to interpret.

Photography in distillery? Yes

Disabled access OK to the visitor centre, but difficult to make the tour.

THE PRODUCT

Malt Glenfarclas

Owner J&G Grant

Region Speyside

Ages Plenty! 10, 12, 15, 17, 21 & 25 years old. (12 and 17 years for export only.)

Water source From the spring on Ben Rinnes, flowing over peat, heather and granite via the Green Burn giving an acidic tang essential for whisky distilling.

Malting Lightly peated malt comes from Arbroath and is introduced to yeast from Menstrie near Stirling.

Bond Ten warehouses on site covered in

black lichen, but as yet no access for visitors, although the filling of casks can be viewed.

Casks Ex-oloroso sherry used up to three times. No cooperage on site now.

Bottling At Broxburn, near Edinburgh.

Experts' opinion 'It goes down singing hymns', a famous taster once said. Other experts speak of a delicate sweet and fruity nose with a full-bodied taste that is sherry-sweet, long and characterful.

Our dram We sampled the 10 year old which has a soft 'sherry' flavour – not too peaty. In the end we bought a 21 year old which, for the price, is a seriously smooth dram.

An excellent detailed explanation with every part of the process carefully covered. Lots of relevant facts and figures; even the awkward questions pleasantly fielded by a guide steeped in whisky lore. Groups are kept small, the tour route is well-planned and quiet spots are used for imparting information. A feeling of being entertained as a guest rather than herded like a highland coo.

Special features The biggest mashtun (33ft/10m in diameter) on Speyside in spotless stainlesss steel and six of the highest and largest copper-lacquered stills in the area immediately catch the eye. The 12 stainless steel washbacks are less glamorous than wooden ones, but are claimed to be cleaner and more economical. Ah well, that's progress for you. Space-age control panels rub shoulders with the traditional spirit safe – large and splendidly set on a wooden base. The malt dresser and the destoner also catch the eye – no less than 4.4lb/2kg of stones are taken out of every 30-tonne load! The huge mashtun takes 15 tonnes of grist at a time and the resultant wash fills two of the 12 washbacks which at least have wooden lids! The washbacks replaced wooden ones in 1973. The stillroom started off with two stills, increased to four in 1960 and to six in 1976. The wash stills are rather double-onioned in shape and all are highly lacquered. Four stills are in use at one time and they are the largest on Speyside.

Access Lots of steel steps but plenty of space and a light, airy, feeling.

Visual impact Spick and span. The stillroom a nice mix of technology and craftsmanship. A good place to be.

Range Whisky, still-shaped decanters, glasses, high-quality branded clothing – hats, jumpers and fleeces.

Style Warm, Scottish, and bright – 'heathery' in tone – sounds kitsch but it ain't.

Staff Ready to help and advise.

Catering None – however a glass of water is always available – it is so good the distillery houses have it on tap!

Toilets Modern and clean. Disabled loo sports a 'bonus' mural from the artist who did pictures in the visitor centre. It features parrots – almost certainly not indigenous to Speyside! **Parent and baby** – space in ladies' loo.

A friendly Highland welcome in a lovely setting and an excellent tour have to be set against a higher than average cost, and nowhere for a bite or an after-tour cuppa. Overall a pretty positive experience, and a good place to visit either as a first experience or to add to one's trophies from the trail.

Overall rating

GLENFIDDICH

The first-ever visitor centre with good facilities but suffers from accommodating too many visitors ... a wee bit 'packaged'. Excellent for foreign visitors. Bottling plant a bonus.

On a pleasant site just outside Dufftown, the heart of the distillery for the visitor is the original plant built by the the Grants in 1886-7. Reception, warehouse, and malt barn (now the dram room) are set attractively round a courtyard decorated with a mass of flowers. An excellent shop situated in the former 'marrying' warehouse completes a pleasant group of buildings of real Scottish character.

Established 1886-7

Enquiries 01340 820373

Website www.glenfiddich.com

Opening hours Mid-Oct to Easter, Mon-Fri, 9.30am-4.30pm; Easter to mid-Oct, Mon-Sat, 9.30am-4.30pm; Easter to mid-Oct, Sun, 12-4.30pm.

Getting there On the A941 half-a-mile (800m) north of Dufftown.

Parking/reception Generous parking area with toilets, picnic tables on the right as you enter. Reception is a spacious room and the-atre in the original distillery building, well set out with a guide always on hand to give a friendly greeting. The new film (2000) lasts 18 minutes, and compared to the previous one is mildly disappointing. While there are lovely views, vivid colours and rather loud music, there is not much content apart from a hard-sell for Glenfiddich. Could the creators of the original distillery visitor centre be losing their once sure touch?

Tour frequency On demand.

Maximum group size 15.

Cost Free.

Group bookings By appointment: many coaches roll up every day.

Visual aids 18 minute film in theatre – headphones for all – in English, French, German, Spanish, Italian and Japanese.

Foreign visitors Guides speak French, German, Italian and Spanish. This is a big plus.

Photography in distillery? Yes

Disabled access To reception, video, ground floor of stillroom, warehouse and malt barn.

THE PRODUCT

Malt Glenfiddich

Owner William Grant & Sons

Region Speyside

Ages 'No age', 12, 15, 18, 21 & 30 years old.

Water source The Robbie Dhu Spring.

Malting Carried out at Portgordon on the Moray Firth.

Bond Viewing area in traditional warehouse with the 'marrying' vat. Ther are no less than 38 modern warehouses in the area.

Casks 90% ex-bourbon.

Bottling Uniquely on site at Glenfiddich – a fascinating sight with automated lines and hand-packing in tin drums and boxes. After the army of stills come bottles apparently drilled like lines of infantry!

Experts' opinion Straw/gold in colour, light well-balanced with a sweet follow-through and a soft maltiness at the end. One of the finest Speysides, now sold in 180 countries.

Our dram Free, but still a wee bit of a let-down to be offered either an unaged malt (pleasant but anonymous) or a honey liqueur. With so many magnificent Glenfiddichs around a wee temptation would not go amiss. We adore the Solera Reserve 15 year old. Plans are afoot for a sampling room where drams will be full and varied but understandably not free.

Glenfiddich is perhaps the victim of its own success – it is plenty busy and lacking a little in spontaneity. Visitors miss out on quite a lot – milling, (no samples of malt and grist), no cask filling, no cooperage (although it is still done on site), and you are too distant from the multiple and elegant spirit safes to see the spirit flowing through them. What you do see is impressive enough which makes up for a lot. The bottling and packing building is a strong finish to the tour.

Special features The contrast between two large 10-tonne mashtuns with copper covers (one raised for visitors to peer in) and 13 Glenfiddich-style small stills, all in the same hall, is arresting. Nearby are 24 washbacks in Oregon Douglas fir – an impressive array. There are five copper wash stills with long narrow swan necks, and eight spirit stills, all nicely shaped with copper condensers behind them – like a little army on parade. All are still coal-fired. The guide told us that there are a further 15 stills in another hall! The bottling plant is great fun for young and old alike – a fascinating mix of automation and manual labour to a precise orderly rhythm.

Access Restricted to mashtun, washbacks, stillhouse, warehouse and bottling. It is all easy and straightforward.

Visual impact A bit old-fashioned with well-worn areas. Mashtuns and stills in one big area make a positive impression. The size of the groups means it can be difficult to see and hear. Entering through the stillroom first tends to get visitors out of sequence with the process, as does passing through again en-route to the washbacks – it takes a good guide to overcome the layout problems.

SHOP

Range Comprehensive – indoor and outdoor branded clothing with fitting rooms, whisky, confectionery, rugs, rucksacks – a first-class facility like a posh department store – more Jenners' than C&A.

Style Separate shop pleasantly appointed and attractive, if a mite pricey.

Staff Part of the department store ethos – friendly but detached.

Catering Tea, coffee, packets of shortbread and whisky cake in the malt barn where you have your dram. It is not very well publicised and you could miss it.

Toilets In the malt barn and car park. Undistinguished but clean. Disabled loos in also in the malt barn and car park. **Parent and baby** – in the ladies' toilet in the malt barn.

SUMMARY

Glenfiddich started the fashion for tours and visitor centres and has over 125,000 visitors a year. There is much to enjoy and the service for foreign visitors is superb, but, sadly, the tour is no longer the best nor indeed the most comprehensive. What you get is a good honest reliable experience, at no charge, but for the individual visitor, perhaps a little bit too processed and packaged.

Overall rating

GLEN GRANT

This has everything – pretty setting, good friendly tour, lots to see, and the garden in the glen. A visit and a dram to savour.

Tucked away in the glen surrounded by trees, this is an archetypal distillery with some handsome buildings and 'wee Geordies' still in the courtyard. The highlight is the gardens – 22 acres of lovely restored Victoriana – wide and open at first then narrowing to a little path up to where Major Grant once secreted in a rock-face safe a dram for guests who made it that far. In summer you may have your dram in his summerhouse, still complete with staghorn chandelier.

Established 1840

Enquiries 01542 783318

Website None

Opening hours Mid-Mar to end-Oct, Mon-Sat, 10am-4pm; Sun, 11.30am-4pm; Jun-end Sept, Mon-Sat 10.30am-5pm; Sun, 11.30am-5pm.

Getting there At the north end of Rothes on the A491 at the roundabout. Bus service from Elgin passes close by.

Parking/reception Park on the right. (Disabled go straight ahead into courtyard.) Lovely approach through the woods and across burn to splendid visitor centre (1996). It is light and airy with a style more modern than most in colour and lighting, reflecting the best of Italian design. At reception, shop display and sales are all in one place and things can get a bit crowded. Good video of the garden restoration (1993-1996) whiles away the minutes before tour starts.

Tour frequency On demand

Maximum group size 10

Cost £2.50. Redeemable in shop. Under-18s are free. No under-8s allowed in the distillery.

Group bookings Coaches and groups by prior arrangement.

Visual aids Boards at key points, a model and good videos in exhibition area and Major Grant's (reconstructed) study.

Foreign visitors Display boards in French, German, Italian and Spanish (earphones for video).

Photography in distillery? No

Disabled access To visitor centre, stillroom and Major Grant's study. Best of all, during the summer months, a chauffeur-driven buggy will whisk you up the garden for your dram – a superb service.

THE PRODUCT

Malt Glen Grant

Owner Seagram Distillers (in sale process)

Region Speyside, but there are some who prefer Highland!

Ages No age given, 5, 8 & 10 years old.

Water source Caperdonich Springs in the gardens.

Malting Carried out by Paul's of Buckie.

Bond Cask filling at Keith: access to viewing area in a traditional warehouse.

Casks 5 & 8 year old aged in ex-bourbon, 10 year old in ex-sherry.

Bottling At Newbridge, Edinburgh.

Experts' opinion (10 year old) – light dry bouquet, light fruity traces, creamy – definitely a pre-dinner dram.

Our dram As it was not high summer we had our potation in Major Grant's study – a reconstruction complete with safari gear. As you sit and sip, an oil painting on the wall rather spookily comes to life with a seven-minute video about the major – a keen if not modest sportsman! The dram is either 'no age given' which is light, sweetish and pleasant (they mix it with coke or apple juice in Italy), or the 10 year old: light in colour, mature, smooth (very) and in its own way a superb dram – clean, mellow and distinctive.

A good tour, informative, easy to follow, with a nice touch of humour. What you don't see (milling, casking) is well explained and illustrated. It's a pity visitors are kept a little at arm's length at the four spirit safes (by McMillan of Prestonpans) which are particularly splendid. Questions are well-fielded and answers to really obscure ones are found quickly. Well-shepherded with plenty of space and good views – especially in the stillroom – which is viewed both from above and later at furnace level. No herding, and nice pace.

Special features Everything about Glen Grant is big – starting with a 12-tonne stainless steel mashtun with an impressive underback, followed by 10 capacious washbacks in Oregon pine, now 45 years old. The well-lit stillroom boasts eight lacquered stills with brass hatches – four almost mushroom-shaped wash stills with curved and narrow swan necks and four spirit stills with a wee 'mini-onion' – nice sexy curves abound. Unique to Glen Grant are copper spirit purifiers en route to the condensers which are stationed outside. The purifiers are part of the mystique – imparting lightness and encouraging early maturation – according to our guide.

Access Good and well-planned. Minor reservations about lack of access to the milling area and the spirit safes are a bit far away for comfort.

Visual impact The stillroom is the high-point – and of course the gardens. The former is bright and smart and the latter perfectly groomed.

Range Glen Grant malts, garden bits and bobs, books, truffles, lovat shades of Peter Scott knitwear, golf balls, and nice perspex dram trays.

Style In the visitor centre – lovely mix of cream wood and stainless steel, all backlit to show off the pale hue of Glen Grant to perfection.

Staff Friendly – usually your guide will have a lovely Speyside accent.

Catering None on site – try the plain loaf at Simpson's the baker's in Rothes – spread with home-made raspberry jam on a thick layer of butter: a 'jeely-piece' fit for a king – or Major Grant's aristocratic guests.

Toilets Colour-coded and well-signposted! Immaculate. Good loos for the disabled. **Parent and baby** – no facilities

This is an experience any visitor will enjoy. The setting is quite splendid, the tour better than average, the folk friendly and devoted, and the gardens are simply not to be missed, especially if you have your dram there. Strongly recommended for the disabled – you can see more of the tour than most places, enjoy good videos and, best of all, savour that buggy ride through the gardens.

Overall rating

GLENLIVET

State-of-the-art visitor centre. A warm welcome, first-class tour. Superb setting. Equally good for first-timers or seasoned campaigners.

After that spectacular drive up the valley of the River Livet, one finds the distillery nestling in the hillside, with its own working farm, complete with Highland cows and a pond with white ducks. The outstanding Minmore House hotel is adjacent to the distillery. Oystercatchers nest on pebbles beside one of the many outbuildings, jealously guarded by distillery staff. Grass and flower beds abound, immaculately tended by escapees from the stillroom and tun room. If the gods have restricted you to visiting one distillery, this could be a wise choice.

Established 1824

Enquiries 01542 783220

Website www.glenlivet.com

Opening hours Apr-Oct, Mon-Sat, 10am-4pm; Sun, 12.30pm-4pm; Jul-Aug, Mon-Sat, 10am-6pm; Sun, 12.30pm-6pm

Getting there Four miles (6.4km) south of Bridge of Avon (A95) on the B9008 turn right for Tomintoul and then left after 150yd/135m, at the primary school. The road is down a beautiful glen beside the River Livet – look out for malt lorries on the bends.

Parking/reception Follow the signs to large car park at visitor centre and a lovely, welcoming smile from a tartan-clad lass. Completed in 1997 in an existing building, the facility is bang up to date. In an open-plan area you will find reception, shop and café. Downstairs there is an interactive exhibition on the history of Glenlivet and its founder, the redoubtable George Smith.

This area is so pleasant you have to positively wrench yourself away for the tour!

Tour frequency Every 15-20 mins as required.

Maximum group size 12

Cost £3. Redeemable in shop. Under-18's are free. Under-8s not admitted.

Group bookings By appointment.

Visual aids The exhibition is a dramatic multi-media presentation of the history of the glen, its people, and its distillery. Characters spring to life as you pass. Press buttons and the process of distilling is laid out step-by-step. Finally, float into a sensuous cinema, all light, colour and sound – and contained inside a washback to boot!

Foreign visitors Wall-mounted boards in French, German, Italian and Spanish.

Photography in distillery? No

Disabled access Tours are not possible for the disabled.

THE PRODUCT

Malt	The Glenlivet
Owner	Seagram Distillers (in sale process)
Region	Speyside
Ages	12, 18 & 21 years old

Water source From Josie's Well which never runs dry.

Malting Malt from Paul's of Buckie, lightly peated and delivered in 400-tonne loads.

Bond Ten warehouses with a capacity of 65,000 barrels.

Casks Predominantly ex-bourbon (12 year old), and predominantly ex-sherry (18 year old). The spirit matured in this mix of casks is then 'married' to the perfect consistency of taste and colour at Keith.

Bottling At Paisley near Glasgow.

Experts' opinion A first-class malt, one of the world's great whiskies. Sherry-cask sweet on the palate with hints of honey. A very smooth dram and perhaps the archetypal Speyside dram.

Our dram A choice of 12 and 18 year old and the new 12 year old finished in French oak. This last is superb – complex, rich, fragrant. The 18 year old has all that one expects from a Glenlivet – rich, mellow, deep amber, eminently potable.

TOUR EXPERIENCE

Arguably it gets no better than this – clear, full of memorable facts, logical and lots of friendly humour. Every question was dealt with expertly to the benefit of the whole group. Take this tour and you will know all you'll ever need to know – who says learning can't be fun? The route is well thought out, easy to follow, and visually satisfying. One feels cossetted, certainly not squeezed through a sausage machine as is sadly sometimes the case.

Special features An immaculate maroon milling machine over 40 years old, then the tunroom with a stainless steel mashtun. Next are eight nicely set washbacks built in Oregon pine leading on to four pairs of lacquered copper stills of elegant proportions with long necks and lyne arms. They accompany two gleaming spirit safes in a stillroom which positively glows in elegant fitness for its purpose. There are ten warehouses with a capacity of 65,000 barrels on site. Visitors are taken to one where casks are stored on modern steel racking, piled higher than normal but still set on earthen floors. A church window at the end of the warehouse sets the tone for viewing this sanctuary.

Access In all directions and areas but easy, safe, and beautifully clean.

Visual impact This place is loved and cared for. Exciting, colourful and as romatic as a 'factory' can be. You can see the hi-tech at work, but sense that the art and craft is still there in spades.

SHOP

Range Whiskies from the owner group, books, tapes, CDs, glasses, Glenlivet clothing, rucksacks, film and shortbread.

Style Themed in green, a triumph in design, seductive and very debilitating for the money clip.

Staff Well-trained, helpful, attentive.

Catering Bright with an attractive range of sandwiches, pastries and hot snacks till 3pm, all served with a ready smile. The coffee is superb and if you must have beer or wine in a distillery, you can.

Toilets State of the art. Palatial loos for the disabled – the visitor centre is accessible separately from the exhibition. **Parent and baby** – no facilities – but there are high chairs in the café.

SUMMARY

This is as good as it gets, and that's pretty good. The ambience is right, the welcome sincere, the visuals superb, and the tour a joy to savour. Round off the experience with a broccoli quiche (to-die-for) in the café, and drive back down the glen, a better person for your visit.

Overall rating

GLEN MORAY

Friendly and informal. Authoritative, comprehensible tour. No frills but bags of atmosphere. Underplayed but not to be undervalued.

Built originally as a brewery in the classic, square, layout of a Scottish farm, there is a courtyard surrounded by traditional, low-ceilinged, row-of-cottage warehouses. In a little valley on the edge of Elgin, Glen Moray is cosy and intimate, just like the welcome. Part of the Glenmorangie plc stable, Glen Moray now boasts Ardbeg as a sister distillery.

Established 1897

Enquiries 01343 542577

Website www.glenmoray.com

Opening hours All year, Mon-Fri, 9.30am-4pm.

Getting there From A96 in Elgin, take the B9010 signposted Dallas, just past the hospital. Carry straight on at a roundabout into Pluscarden Road, then first right into Fleurs Drive. Distillery is on right at first bend.

Parking/reception On the right at reception. Likely to be expanded for 2001 season. Reception is in a wee cottagey place on the left as you enter. There are no frills here but some of the nicest people in the industry, led by manager Ed Dodson and visitor centre manager Tracey Davidson – what a welcome! Soon you are off on tour with one of seven of the ten working staff who take visitors around. Boy, do they know their stuff – this is really from the horse's mouth, and from seriously dedicated guys who take great pride in keeping the distillery looking its very best. They don't intend to be overshadowed by their allegedly more 'glam' sister-distilleries at Glenmorangie and Ardbeg.

Tour frequency 9.30am, 10.30am, 11.30am, 1.30pm, 2.30pm, 3.30pm.

Maximum group size Eight

Cost £2.00. Redeemable in shop.

Group bookings Small groups by arrangement.

Visual aids None. Who needs them with guides like these!

Foreign visitors You'll need to understand English!

Photography in distillery? Yes

Disabled access No facilities. If you contact Tracey, a modified tour can be arranged.

THE PRODUCT

Malt Glen Moray

Owner Glenmorangie plc

Region Speyside

Ages The Introductory, 12 & 16 years old.

Water source From the River Lossie.

Malting From various sources including Paul's of Buckie and Simpsons of Berwick-on-Tweed.

Bond Excellent visit to old and new warehouses and the cask-filling room.

Casks Ex-bourbon and sherry.

Bottling At the company's own bottling plant at Broxburn, West Lothian.

Experts' opinion Amber and gold in colour, fresh, medium-bodied with a sweet apple hint, round and fruity, a touch of vanilla. A superb dram.

Our dram Choose from The Introductory, which spends six months in a Chardonnay wine cask, and the 12 and 16 which spend a similar time in hand-picked Chenin Blanc wine casks from the Loire Valley. If the 16 year old is anything to go by, this really lifts an already superb malt. A fresh heather-honey nose with a dry, fruity, taste. We had to have a bottle. Look out for them in Black Watch or Cameron Highlander tins, while stocks last.

This is the best of its kind – authentic and informed. And that's from the man who works the mash-tun and the still! There is some debunking of the tourist myths perpetuated elswhere and not before time. Our 'guide' Bill was a delight with the technical questions you dare not ask at other places. The tour is comprehensive, thorough, well-organised and gives a clear picture. One of the few you could tackle twice in a day! Small groups are the secret, as is enthusiasm – more like a family outing than a guided tour.

Special features The milling process (another big Porteous job) was well-explained in every detail, complete with the sieves to measure the correct proportions of husk, grist and flour – reassuringly lo-tech. The stainless steel mashtun (Newmills of Elgin) and the five, dull, steel washbacks look ordinary, but the explanation of how they work isn't – it is riveting. The four copper stills are spectacular when first seen from below, while the diagrams on the control panel enable visitors to have a crystal-clear picture of distillation from wash to finished spirit. Another highlight is the contrast between a modern seven-tier warehouse, and a traditional three-tier version. Pity the stencil markings on the ends of the barrels are being replaced by bar-codes. How dull!

Access Good, but plenty of stairs to deal with. You get a chance to see everything.

Visual impact Relatively modern with little wood or embellishment, but loved and cherished – seeing the stills from beneath was impressive.

Range Company malts: Glen Moray, Glenmorangie and Ardbeg. Teeshirts, sweat shirts etc.

Style Set in the dram room – homely, relaxed, nicely displayed.

Staff Tracey, the visitor centre manager, is a wonderful hostess. If you are lucky distillery manager Ed Dodson will drop in for a chat – makes you feel a real VIP.

Catering None, but Elgin has all you'll need.

Toilets Like home but even more spotless. No loos for the disabled. **Parent and baby** – no facilities.

Glen Moray is far removed in style and facilities from the mainstream 'tourist' distilleries, but it does provide a first-class, well-balanced tour with lots to see, answers to all your questions, and a dram of something special at the end. The group owns Ardbeg and Glenmorangie too – do they know about their hidden treasure buried in Elgin?

Overall rating

MACALLAN

For the aficionado, this has everything. Highlight is the inner sanctum where malts are nosed and married.

The Macallan site covers 600 acres overlooking the River Spey with a farm, warehouses, fairly modern distillery buildings, houses and Easter Elchies, a Jacobean tower house. It lies on an ancient drove route and the farm once supplied whisky to passing drovers. Plenty of trees, grass and views especially over the river, but it is not a pretty distillery. A new visitor centre and shop have opened since our visit.

Established 1824

Enquiries 01340 871471

Website www.themacallan.com

Opening hours Al year, Mon-Fri, 9.30am-3pm.

Getting there From the A941 Elgin to Dufftown road, take the B9102 to Archiestown just north of Craigellachie. The distillery is on left after a mile (1.6km) or so.

Parking/reception Follow signs past farm and through distillery. Turn left at roundabout into new car park beside the Gardener's Cottage.There Margaret Gray and her colleagues will greet you like old friends and lead you into a setting of great charm where a relaxed informality soon sets you at ease. Already the unique Macallan confidence – a kind of benign 'whas like us' is evident. Soon the tour is underway, a beguiling mix of history, humour and the lowdown on the distillation of what many buffs rate as the Rolls Royce of malts.

Tour frequency Regular tours but still best to book ahead. Last tour at 3pm.

Maximum group size 10

Cost Free – some things are beyond price!

Group bookings Small and by appointment only .

Visual aids Display boards at key points of the tour. In the silent season. A 'virtual tour' is laid on.

Foreign visitors Leaflets in French, German, Greek, Italian, Spanish and Japanese.

Photography in distillery? Yes

Disabled access Tour is not easy with quite a lot of stairs to negotiate. The new visitor centre includes a nosing room allowing disabled visitors to reach the very heart of Macallan.

THE PRODUCT

Malt   The Macallan

Owner   The Macallan Distillers Ltd

Region   Speyside

Ages   10, 12 (for export), 18, 25 & 30 years old.

Water source Borehole aquifers. Source water is 492ft/150m below ithe surface – soft and pure.

Malting Macallan use Golden Promise – a traditional malting barley from Simpsons at Berwick on Tweed.

Bond 70,000 sherry butts on site of 500 litres (110 gallons) each. Another 80,000 in a new warehouse, racked 11 barrels high.

Casks Only the best European red oak oloroso sherry butts – they are only used twice.

Bottling 'Married' on site, bottled in Drumchapel on the outskirts of Glasgow

Experts' opinion Smooth, fragrant, full-bodied with a hint of apple. The 18 year old is as good as any – a honeyed, wine-like sweet aroma, and a complex combination of spice, sherry, citrus and oak.

Our dram The 10-year-old Macallan, with a dash of water – what can one say – everything you would expect from one of Scotland's top malts. Mahogany in colour, with hints of fruit, and sherry. Smooth as a baby's bottom, lingering aftertaste – can I have another please? 30% of production goes into Famous Grouse – little wonder it is Scotland's best selling blend.

This has everything – clear, meticulous, logical at just the right pace and with lots of interesting asides – history lessons were never like this in school. Soon guests are all questioning and probing (in several languages) a guide whose enthusiasm never flags or wanes ... equalled perhaps, but never bettered. This tour lasts nearly two hours and is not for the casual whiler-away of a dismal Tuesday. But aficionado or tyro, if you have the enthusiasm, don't miss it. There is a fair amount of walking and climbing but you are unobtrusively shepherded, and see and hear everything. Small groups really do make all the difference.

Special features The washbacks – all of them of stainless steel with sealed tops, are more factory than fantasy. Most unusually the stillroom has five huge wash stills, feeding 10 much smaller spirit stills. All have rather steep necks as the spirit vapour is encouraged to fall over to the condensers without lingering. These curiously 'small' stills of traditional onion shape are the smallest direct-fired stills in Scotland. The spirit from these is fuller and has more body than normal. The bonded warehouse is crammed with interest, with full access and an invitation to 'nose' the contents of a barrel and identify the aromas. In no time at all the real tour de force – a visit to the inner sanctum of the head 'noser' Bob Delgano – a cross between a chemist's shop, a science lab and a wizard's lair. The secrets of consistency (or some of them) are revealed. It takes a panel of nosers days to select no less than 50 butts to give the classic nose, taste and colour to each batch. Nowhere else in the world of distilling can the visitor come so close to understanding the art of malt whisky perfection.

Access The milling process is considered too dusty and noisy, but we saw everything else, including a hot and noisy stillroom. Access stairs are metal and safe.

Visual impact Much more up-to-date than expected, but with no maltings. A huge modern stillhouse with acres of glass and no less than 15 stills.

Range Whisky, marmalade, umbrellas and baseball caps.

Style State-of-the-art decor and lighting. A bare stone gable houses a mouth-watering but expensive display of rare old Macallan.

Staff Your tour guide is all the staff you'll ever need!

Catering None provided, but hotels in Craigellachie nearby and café at the Speyside Cooperage

Toilets Immaculate for all. **Parent and baby** – no facilities.

The Macallan has (by design) only a few thousand visitors a year and they are treated to a superb tour. But it is not a beginner's tour – build up to this one, if and when you have survived a few less demanding tours. This is not the most easy-on-the-eye of distilleries, but after it you will be a true graduate in the appreciation of one of the finest malts.

Overall rating

Connoisseurs' choice. To be lingered over and savoured from start to finish. Unique do-it-yourself tour.

Close to the town centre beside the River Isla and surrounded by trees, Strathisla lays claim to being the prettiest of distilleries, with its twin pagodas, water wheel and handsomely proportioned stone buildings set in cobbled yards. It looks, as indeed it is, the oldest operating distillery in the Highlands. It has worn extraordinarily well.

Established 1786

Enquiries 01542 783044

Website www.chivas.com

Opening hours Apr 1 to Oct 31, Mon-Sat, 10am-5pm; Sun, 12-4pm; Sep-Easter, Mon-Fri, 10am-4pm

Getting there Keith is on the main trunk A96 Aberdeen to Inverness Road. The distillery lies in Seafield Avenue, directly off the main road. It is a few minutes walk from a bus route and a similar distance from Keith Station.

Parking/reception Car park is tight and sloping, across the road from the distillery. Reception comprises an area with the atmosphere of an upmarket Victorian accountants' office with elegant furniture, plenty of space and a wee window at which to buy your tour ticket. Here one learns that this is a DIY tour with help from staff and a guide-book. Next door is the Isla room, (an elegant club-style lounge) where coffee and shortbread are served as you sink into luxurious chairs and settees to master the guide book. An elegant and pleasant start to the tour.

Tour frequency As you wish after coffee and a browse of the tour book.

Maximum group size 20

Cost £4.00. Redeemable in shop. Under-18's are free. Under-8's not allowed in distillery.

Group bookings By appointment. Over 25 get 10% discount.

Visual aids The book has it all. In the distillery all the key features are labelled and even the pipes are colour coded.

Foreign visitors Guide book in French, German, Spanish, Italian, Japanese: some hostesses speak European languages.

Photography in distillery? No

Disabled access Even the public rooms are a little difficult. The distillery visit is daunting.

THE PRODUCT

Malt   Strathisla

Owner   Seagram Distillers (in sale process)

Region   Speyside

Age   12 years old

Water source The Fons Bullions spring in the gardens across the road from the distillery.

Malting Carried out by Paul's of Buckie, lightly peated to Strathisla's unique specification.

Bond After inspecting the cask filling store there is access to a stone warehouse with barrels traditionally racked.

Casks Ex-sherry and bourbon.Filled in Keith.

Bottling At Newbridge, Edinburgh.

Experts' opinion Strathisla has a beautiful fruity nose, a long lingering fullness on the palate and a touch of dark, oaky, tannins. An outstanding after-dinner malt. Chivas Regal has a light, lingering, aroma, is smooth and balanced with just a complex hint of smoke. With Strathisla at its heart, it justifies its reputation as a luxury blend.

Our dram Our hostess encouraged us to 'nose' the constituent malts and the grain whisky which together make Chivas Regal. We found the finished product to our liking, smooth and svelte. The malt was of excellent quality – fruity, light and sweet. It's quite hard to get a hold of, but well worth the effort.

TOUR EXPERIENCE

Our hostess prepared us thoroughly and pleasantly and off we went. The route is clear and logical, much is self-explanatory and distillery staff are genuinely willing to explain things as far as their duties allow. We felt relaxed and able to set our own pace, even doubling-back as we felt inclined. Clearly there is no marshalling and the views are unrestricted. Efforts are made to ensure that not too many people are on tour at the same time. It was nice to take time out to watch the River Isla flowing by and to watch coopers re-hooping a washback – hard labour with a whip of metal of such vast circumference.

Special features An immaculate Porteous mill resplendent in maroon. The mashtun is unusual with a raised copper 'roof' and mixing paddles set horizontally on a racked track – old-fashioned but efficient. In the tun room are 10 Oregon-pine washbacks – unusually large gaps in the floor allow one to see their full two-storey stature. There are huge copper pipes with brass valves which look as if they have escaped from the engine room of a Clyde paddle steamer. The stillroom has four slightly shabby workmanlike stills with wide necks and big copper condensers; all smoky and unlacquered with brass labels denoting their manufacture by Grant of Dufftown. They look just right under a dark open-beamed roof. Close by two magnificent brass-bound spirit safes are set on a wooden base.

Another highlight of a memorable visit is the dram room. The former malting floor has been transformed in recent years and now resembles the study or the library of a stately home, opulent but intimate – a perfect place to browse while enjoying a generous dram of 12-year-old Strathisla or the similarly aged Chivas Regal, in many eyes Scotland's premier blend.

Access A fair amount of climbing up and down, some narrowish stairs, but safety is clearly of great importance and there are no uncharted hazards.

Visual impact A compact working distillery, clean, well-maintained with a lot to see.

SHOP

Range Whiskies from the owning group, decanters, glasses, miniatures, jewellery, shortbread (as consumed with the coffee), umbrellas, keyrings, fashion goods and more.

Style Maroon and wood panelling complement the chic of lounge and library.

Staff Friendly and even willing to gift-wrap any item purchased in the shop and at no extra charge.

Catering There is no cafeteria, but the coffee and shortbread make all the difference.

Toilets Of the highest standard and elegance, matching the splendour of the Isla room and the dram rooms. **Parent and baby** – no facilities

SUMMARY

If you want a casual introduction to whisky on a wet afternoon, go elsewhere. Come to Strathisla if you want to be educated, enlightened and cossetted in a whirl of sensuous and sensual pleasure. You'll depart a happier and a wiser person, anxious to return if only to buy another bottle and tuck in to a reprise of the coffee and the delectable shortbread.

Overall rating

SPEYSIDE COOPERAGE

This is magic – the art of coopering with the sweat and toil before your very eyes. Excellent visitor facilities.

A lovely setting. The attractive visitor centre, café, shop, workshop and mountains of casks and fresh wood are all set on a hillside with fields and woods in every direction. Once every Scotch whisky distillery maintained its own cooperage but now very few do and the Speyside Cooperage has become a increasingly vital part of the whisky trade in Scotland.

Established 1947. Visitor centre in 1992.

Enquiries 01340 871108

Website None

Opening hours All year, Mon-Fri, 9am-4.30pm; Jun-Sep, Sat, 9.30am-12.30pm.

Getting there On the A941 Craigellachie to Dufftown road, a quarter of a mile (400m) south of Craigellachie.

Parking/reception Good, big, car park on right of entrance. Disabled parking straight on at the visitor centre A warm welcome and an explanation that the tour has three parts – the history display in the foyer, a 10-minute video next door, and finally the viewing gallery above. A promise of a free tasting is designed to entice you in due course over to the elegant shop across the garden.

Tour frequency Every 10 mins

Maximum group size No limit

Cost Adults, £2.95. Concessions, £2.45. Children, £1.75. Family ticket, £7.95.

Group bookings Parties of over 15, £2.25 per person.

Visual aids Excellent display on the history of coopering and a good video on the traditions of the trade.

Foreign visitors Displays and video in French, German, Italian, Spanish and Japanese

Photography in distillery? Yes

Disabled access Disabled visitors have access to the visitor centre, video and shop, but not the viewing gallery. There is a book of pictures for them to peruse.

THE PRODUCT

New casks for brewers and refurbished ones for the Scotch whisky industry. Every shape and size imaginable is can be catered for but the basic activity of the cooperage is to import American-sized barrels as flatpacks and rebuild these into UK-sized casks by reworking the staves. In this way, for every five American flatpacks imported, four UK-sized casks can be manufactured.

Cask sizes range as follows:

Spanish sherry **butt** (500 litres/110 gallons)

Hogshead (250-305 litres/55-67 gallons)

American **Barrel** (173-191 litres/38-42 gallons)

The **Quarter** (127-159 litres/28-35 gallons)

The **Octave** (45-68 litres/10-15 gallons).

There are guides waiting in the viewing gallery who are friendly and helpful. You can witness whisky barrels being refurbished and repaired – re-hooping, new ends, reed seals, fresh paint – the lot. Hard work carried out with consummate skill.

Special features Made us feel quite exhausted just spectating. Apprentices can be seen serving their time in the traditional manner. It reminds the visitor of a bygone age where craftsmanship was at a premium but hard labour was the price which had to be paid. With so few distilleries now doing their own coopering – Glenfiddich and Loch Lomond still do – this is where to see a part of the whisky process which is no longer a common sight. Some 80 distilleries use Speyside Cooperage's services – 100,000 bourbon and sherry casks are overhauled each year between their 15-year 'shifts'. With sherry casks costing as much as £400 each, distilleries are turning more to bourbon casks which the cooperage trims to UK sizes. After three to five recyclings barrels can end up in gardens, or even as the woodchips which flavour Scottish smoked salmon! 100,000 new barrels are made, with some automation in the process, for brewers.

Access You can see it all from the gallery.

Visual impact Stunning close-ups of a traditional hard-sweat craft.

SHOP

Range Cooperage-related items from barrel garden furniture to miniature casks, whisky souvenirs as in most distillery shops, plus wines, books, tapes and ornaments.

Style Recently extended, a beautiful white building, well-lit with wood, attractively laid out.

Staff Always ready to advise and assist.

Catering Attached to the shop, a café with coffee, tea, soft drinks and shortbread. There is an attractive open veranda with barrel tables and chairs. In the café you are offered a free sample of products matured in Speyside casks – whisky and liqueurs.

Toilets Excellent, clean. Disabled loos are the same. **Parent and baby** – in the ladies' facility

SUMMARY

Sadly there are few distilleries where you can see coopers at work, although some have displays and videos. Nowadays by far the best way to see how this ancient craft is practised is to come here. It completes the distillery experience and is a positive pleasure in its own right. It is perhaps a little too touristy in style, but is not to be missed.

Overall rating

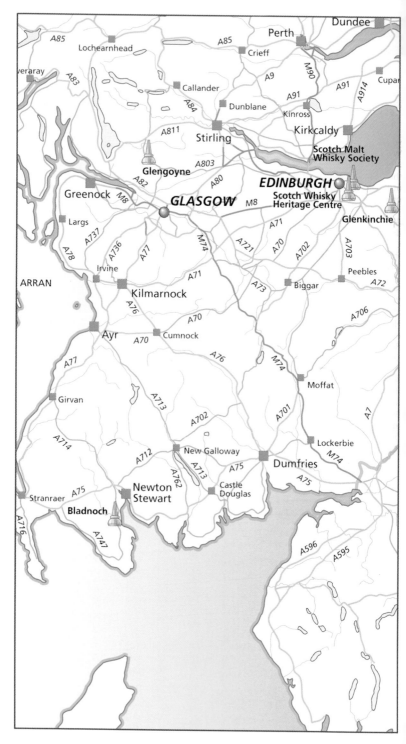

The Lowlands

The three distilleries, the Scotch Whisky Heritage Centre (SWHC) and the Scotch Malt Whisky Society (SMWS) which make up this group are pretty disparate and best tackled separately, although you can make a morning of the SWHC, have a very fine lunch in their Whisky Bond Bistro, and follow that with a visit to the SMWS in the afternoon, but as the latter is a members-only facility, you need to be the guest of a member or willing to join at the time of your visit. We made a rather a pleasant day of a morning at the SWHC with a memorable afternoon visit to Glenkinchie Distillery in East Lothian.

A visit to Bladnoch should really be part of a sampling of the unsung delights of Galloway. Start with coffee at the Old Schoolhouse beyond Castle Douglas on the A75, lunch at the Bladnoch Inn across the road from the distillery, and then dine, wine and stay over at the atmospheric Steampacket Inn at the Isle of Whithorn (01988 500334).

Bookworms should not miss Scotland's only official Booktown which is Wigtown – another Hay-on-Wye in the making. Bikers will enjoy a night at the atmospheric Murray Arms in the High Street of Gatehouse of Fleet (01557 814207). Here, in the room directly on the left as you enter, Robert Burns penned the words to Scot's Wha Hae, inspired by Robert the Bruce's pre-match pep talk to his army before proud Edward's army was sent packing at Bannockburn.

A visit to Glengoyne is inextricably linked in our minds with the lure of the Trossachs and Loch Lomond – what finer prospect for a Sunday afternoon drive from Glasgow or Stirling? Have lunch either at the Black Bull in Killearn (01360 550215) – excellent fare, good conservatory – or at the Buchanan Arms in Drymen (01360 660588), which revived memories of motoring 'adventures' in the 1950s in a none-too-reliable Standard 14 with idiosyncratic Bendix brakes.

BLADNOCH

GLENGOYNE

GLENKINCHIE

SCOTCH MALT
WHISKY SOCIETY

SCOTCH WHISKY
HERITAGE CENTRE

BLADNOCH

Enterprising rebirth of a Galloway legend. Walks, picnics and a super shop.

Standing right beside the river of the same name, Bladnoch comprises of a set of fine grey-stone buildings with slate roofs and an authentic pagoda malting kiln. The distillery makes an attractive picture, especially from the other side of the river with the bridge included. Visitors can picnic at tables by the water, or walk through Collard Wood with its wild orchids – a pleasant place to be on a summer's day. A hospitality room with natural stone walls and roof beams is much in demand for functions and book launches associated with nearby Wigtown, Scotland's Booktown.

Established 1817

Enquiries 01988 402605

Website www.bladnoch.co.uk

Opening hours Easter-end-Oct, Mon-Fri, 9am-5pm; Jul-Aug, Sun 12-5pm; Nov-Easter, contact reception.

Getting there From Newton Stewart take the A714 to Wigtown; before entering the town bear right on to the A746. The distillery is a short distance on the right just before the bridge across the River Bladnoch.

Parking/reception Ample parking in front of distillery. An entrance on the right leads to a reception room with modern toilets and displays – a diagram with lights on the distilling process catches the eye. From there make your way through to the spacious shop, where a really warm Galloway welcome awaits.

Tour frequency Every 15 minutes or so from 10am.

Maximum group size 20

Cost £1.

Group bookings By advance arrangement with distillery reception.

Visual aids Display boards at keypoints. Video after the tour in the dram room. It outlines the history and process of distilling and has a lively commentary.

Foreign visitors Leaflets in shop in French, German and Italian.

Photography in distillery? Yes

Disabled access Everything which is on the ground floor (excepting the mashtun and washbacks) can be accessed.

THE PRODUCT

Malt Bladnoch

Owner Co-ordinated Development Services Ltd

Region Lowland

Age 12 years old

Water source The River Bladnoch above the tidal limit.

Malting Traditionally carried out by Simpsons of Berwick and lightly peated.

Bond Access to one of the 13 warehouses on site where visitors can see casks (with old candleabra sitting atop), coopering implements and artefacts ranging from barrels to stencils and reeds for caulking.

Casks Ex-bourbon and sherry.

Bottling Plenty of time to mull over where the next batch will be bottled in ten years or so. Currently Signatory bottle some of the existing Bladnoch stocks in Edinburgh.

Experts' opinion A light, fresh, delicately peated nose with a dry taste and a fruity richness. Full and stimulating. A touch of perfume to the finish.

Our dram Served from the sideboard in the dram room which has a nice lived-in feel to it, the dram is generous (bottled by Gordon & MacPhail) very light in colour, delicate, a little dry, and a wee touch peaty. It has the colour and character to match its birthplace ... warm and friendly.

A good logical tour – apart from starting rather than ending with a warehouse visit – overall it is well planned and comprehensive. Clear explanations and noticeably knowledgeable responses to questions. Unobtrusive shepherding and a nice pace enable all to absorb every detail. It pays to watch one's footing.

Special features You can see all parts of the milling process with a fine grey mill and its ancient wooden grain elevator. A sign tells you that 135 'coups' (or loads) makes up the 5.4 tonnes of grist for a single mash, a process which takes two hours or more. Neither the stainless steel mashtun (with brand new mixing paddles) or its underback can be described as elegant, sitting untidily under a grey, wooden, farm roof. A section of the perforated mashtun floor is laid out for inspection and makes it easy to visualise how the wash filters through the draff. The six Oregon-pine washbacks with their red hoops are eye-catching in the farm-style hall. Floodlights below the mash room floor help to reveal their considerable depth. In the stillroom are two lacquered copper stills manufactured by Blair of Glasgow. They are quite tall with an elegant single-onion lower section. The wash still almost touches the roof and the spirit still has a medium-diameter lyne arm with a slight, but perceptible, kink. Behind the stills are the condensers looking for all the world like two little rockets ready to be launched. The spirit safe, most unusually, is made of stainless steel – typically workmanlike, in the Bladnoch way – as are the spirit receivers, encased in great big girders. Leaving the stillroom, don't miss the display of cooperage and the old ledgers which were once fillen in, one imagines, with quill pens in immaculate copperplate. In the bond, note the old candleabra which were used before electricity and designed to sit atop the barrels as they were dipped.

Access Good open access but the stairs and wide mesh floors need a bit of care.

Visual impact Down to earth and workmanlike. This is as unspoilt as you will get.

Range This is one of the best and biggest distillery shops with high-quality wares – jewellery, glasses, confectionery, leather goods, ties and scarves, woollens, kilts, shortbread etc. Last but not least there is a really good collection of single malts from a wide range of distilleries.

Style Spacious and airy, cream with hardwood floors, nicely laid out with pictures and distillery artefacts.

Staff So helpful and brimming over with enthusiasm for their recently reborn distillery.

Catering None – the Bladnoch Inn across the road serves good, honest fare.

Toilets Loos in reception. Disabled loos in reception, access by ramp, modern and immaculate. **Parent and baby** – no facilities.

Closed seemingly for ever in 1993, the re-opening in July 2000, albeit on a limited scale, is entirely to the credit of Raymond Armstrong a charming, energetic Irishman whose enthusiasm has swept aside all obstacles to our great benefit. Bladnoch has the South-west to itself and is big enough to cope. A visit to this unspoilt traditional distillery is full of spectacle and interest. The shop is well worth a visit on its own and the river and the walk combine to offer a real Galloway treat. Savour the tour, browse the shop and with a delicate dram of Bladnoch in your hand raise your glass in tribute to Raymond and his dedicated band who take care of you.

Overall rating

GLENGOYNE

Handy for Glasgow and the Trossachs, situated in a beautiful wee glen. Excellent tour with nice washbacks and stills.

The distillery, which still looks a bit like the farm it once was, lies on the imaginary line which divides the Highland and Lowland whisky regions. In terms of scenery the site does them both proud. Glengoyne with its neat white buildings, windows edged in grey, is tucked in a fold of the hills in the entrance to a glen which shares its name, below the distinctively shaped Dumgoyne hill. There is an attractive five-minute walk to the wooded waterfall on the Glengoyne burn which once supplied the fine, soft water for distillation. The walk beside and above the burn is a miniature version of the garden walk at Glen Grant in Rothes. Even with the busy road below, the 'Glen of the wild geese' is a lovely and relaxing place to be.

Established 1833

Enquiries 01360 550254

Website None

Opening hours All year, Mon-Sat, 10am-4pm; Sun, 12-4pm.

Getting there A 14-mile (22km) journey from the M8 in Glasgow. Take the A81 slip road to Aberfoyle. Go through Milngavie and Strathblane and the distillery is on the right before the Killearn junction.

Parking/reception On the left of the A81 coming from Glasgow, opposite the distillery entrance on the warehouse road. Park and walk back to the distillery past the shop and up to reception on the right where, after signing in (and paying) you are invited upstairs for a dram of 10 year old while admiring the view of the glen and the water-fall. The room, in pink and cream, is reminis-cent of the mixed lounge in a country golf club. After an excellent video and a first-class introductory talk, the tour begins on the veranda overlooking a pond fed from the burn which acts as a reservoir for cooling water. Did I see a trout rise?

Tour frequency Each hour on the hour.

Maximum group size 16. Bus parties have their own arrangements and tours.

Cost £3.95.

Group bookings Groups of 10 or more by appointment only.

Visual aids An excellent if slightly 'touristy' video and pictures and diagrams en-route.

Foreign visitors Guides speak the main European languages. Shop has books for sale in European languages.

Photography in distillery? Yes

Disabled access A tour can be arranged which covers all but the fermentation, start-ing from an excellent display area set aside for disabled visitors, and all on one level.

THE PRODUCT

Malt Glengoyne

Owner Lang Brothers (Edrington Group)

Region Highland (southern)

Ages 10, 17, 21 & 30 years old

Water source A reservoir two miles away on the slopes of Dumgoyne – soft and peatless.

Malting Traditional Golden Promise barley malted at Carnoustie on Tayside and dried in hot air with no peat smoke.

Bond No access to the warehouses but there is a good display and account of coopering. The bond was once below a Free Church in Glasgow – hence the couplet: *The spirits below were the spirits of wine / The spirits above were the spirits divine.*

Casks Ex-sherry and refill whisky.

Bottling Glasgow.

Experts' opinion Mellow with warm hints of vanilla and a lovely light, fresh, delicate taste. Younger ages are excellent pre-prandial fare. The 30 year old is best saved for later in the evening.

Our dram We started our tour with an excellent 10 year old, unpeated, smooth and mellow if not wildly distinctive. We were later offered a 17 year old in the shop – probably the pick of the bunch – eminently potable, with no dominant flavours – rich in fragrance, light in colour. Moreish.

TOUR EXPERIENCE

This is a high-quality tour, with each stage of distilling clearly explained by knowledgeable guides, brimful of facts and humour. Some good tips such as, 'Cup your hand to catch a sample of the atmosphere in the washback', resulted in the old knockout punch administered by the carbon dioxide! Questions were dealt with competently and patiently. Firm but unobtrusive shepherding ensures that everyone can see, hear and ask. Stopping points are spacious and often afford a bird's eye view.

Special features The stainless steel mashtun is modest in size, and unusually is situated in the still-room. It sports a beautifully shaped copper canopy, complete with a nautical-looking brass porthole. Close by is a grey, tiled room containing six Oregon-pine washbacks which boast brass plates proclaiming that they are 'Clydebuilt' by the Clyde Cooperage. They have unusual 'hoops' – made of solid iron tubing. The stillroom is bright and airy. Its white walls and copper pipes make a handsome backcloth to three copper stills, one a larger wash still with a pronounced double onion and lyne arms to copper condensers. At one time set up for triple distillation, the two smaller 770-gallon (3495-litre) stills now operate in parallel. The tour ends with a display of cooperage which gives a good impression of the real thing now carried out at Lochwinnoch in Renfrewshire.

Access Some narrow and steep stairs, but the layout is compact and the route well thought out.

Visual impact Business-like, traditional, well-maintained with a lot of lovingly burnished copper.

SHOP

Range An excellent display of whiskies, glasses, foods, woollens, CDs etc. Of particular merit is the comprehensive range of books in different languages.

Style Half-museum, half-shop, atmospheric lighting and interesting displays. You can enjoy spending money here.

Staff Helpful folk, happy to go the extra mile and then some more.

Catering None, but the Beech Tree Inn is nearby. A restaurant/conference centre is planned.

Toilets Those in reception are good, but the ones near the disabled room are a bit tatty. No specific toilet provision for the disabled. **Parent and baby** – no facilities.

SUMMARY

The best part of the visit is the tour itself – these guides really do know their stuff and whatever the state of your knowledge, we guarantee it will be significantly enhanced. The distillery itself is compact, traditional and pleasing on the eye: it is just a pity that visitors don't get to see milling or sample the distinctive aura inside a warehouse, but we cavil. This is a great place to take in when exploring the Trossachs and Loch Lomond. It is, of course, eminently worthwhile in its own right, be the visitor tyro or veteran. **NB:** Highly recommended are the nosing sessions, which take place on Wednesdays at 7.30pm, April through to October – booking is essential. DIY nosing kits are available in the shop – it can become quite addictive!

Overall rating

GLENKINCHIE

The complete experience. Who said museums were dull? Super tour with lots of visual delights. Generous drams of a range of top malts – have your chauffeur take you home!

Robert Burns averred that he had never seen such fine 'corn country' as surrounds Glenkinchie even to this day. Others have called the area the larder of Edinburgh. Rural, lush, almost English in aspect, the surroundings are as gentle as the distillery buildings are harsh – all red brick and industrial, with a huge chimney Fortunately there are lots of trees and even a bowling green for the use of distillery staff. The overall attraction lies in the wider horizons, the model-village ambience and the soft outlines of the Lammermuir Hills.

Established 1837

Enquiries 01875 342004

Website www.scotch.com

Opening hours Nov-Feb, Mon-Fri, 11am-3pm; Sun, 11.30am-4pm; June-End Sept, Mon-Sat, 10am-5pm; Sun, 11.30am-5pm.

Getting there Leave Edinburgh on the A68 and after passing through Dalkeith, in a few miles (4km) turn right on to the A6093 for Haddington. In Pencaitland turn right at the brown sign for Glenkinchie Distillery.

Parking/reception Car park on right opposite distillery entrance. Disabled visitors park beside the visitor centre. Reception has an appropriately warehouse ambience – all green cast iron and wood and incorporates the shop. A splendid welcome and then off upstairs to while away the time until the tour in the three extensive galleries of the museum. So much to see it's as well you can go back again after the tour.

Tour frequency Half-hourly.

maximum group size 15

Cost £3.50. Redeemable in shop.

Group bookings By appointment with reception. Coaches park on left before distillery entrance.

Visual aids The museum halls– see under Special Features opposite.

Foreign visitors Leaflets in French, German, Italian, Spanish, Dutch, Japanese. Boards at keypoints on the tour in French, German, Italian and Spanish.

Photography in distillery? Yes

Disabled access To everything except fermentation. There is even a lift to the museum. Staff pride themselves in helping out. Special arrangements for sight -impaired visitors are very good – they are encouraged to feel the model distillery. Visitors can forego the tour, linger in the museum and catch up for the sampling of Glenkinchie.

THE PRODUCT

Malt   Glenkinchie

Owner   UDV

Region   Lowland

Ages   10 years and double-matured.

Water source A spring on site and a reservoir on the neighbouring Lammermuir Hills.

Malting Carried out at Burghead on the Moray Firth. Peat used to come from the Borders when malting was carried out on site.

Bond Warehouses are on site. Access is planned from 2001 onwards. This would fill in the only notable gap in the proceedings.

Casks Ex-bourbon and sherry

Bottling At Leven in Fife. Blending at Kilmarnock in Ayrshire (home of Johnnie Walker) and Shieldhall, Glasgow.

Experts' opinion Light, sweet with a hint of peat on the nose. Dry, malty, spicy, well-balanced and smooth. Definitely pre-dinner – long and lingering.

Our dram This is a classy deal. You start with the 10 year old – pale in colour and oh so delicate, slightly sweet and fruity. A seriously smooth, malty dram. After that, we were invited to try several from a huge range – Mortlach particularly tickled our palates. Belated advice – go by taxi or have one's chauffeur in attendance.

You won't find better – comprehensive, well-planned, with space to see, hear and ask. Clear, lucid, friendly advice from dedicated guides make this a joy to experience. Unobtrusive marshalling at the right pace, with time to savour the details and the mystique. Don't try to 'do' Glenkinchie in a hurry!

Special features The museum halls are your first treat. The first contains murals explaining the process and history, and a 'farm-size' still and washback demonstrating how it all began. Next comes a truly monumental model distillery – we paced it out at 50ft/15.2m long, and some 8ft/2.4m high. Built for the Empire Exhibition at Wembley in 1924 by James Risk, and only rediscovered in 1963, it is perfect in every detail, comprehensively labelled and a must to savour. Last comes a 'period' office complete with quill pens, ledgers and the old accounts laid out. One note tells of 'reduced office hours' of 7am to 6pm weekdays, and seems to expect 'grateful' staff to forego meal-breaks in return for this act of munificence. In the tour assembly area there is an excellent 'touch screen' video about the Classic Malts, but confusingly it is only the one on a central plinth that has any effect. The recently revealed kiln and fan show what it used to be like – all smoke and peat. Next is the resplendent Porteous mill with a wooden grain elevator dating from 1890, then via the Abercrombie steel mashtun and past the huge 'shift' bell. On to six Oregon-pine washbacks, dark in colour with green hoops, where fermentation takes all of 60-72 hours (elsewhere it can be as little 48). A unique feature is the open mixing tank for yeast prior to its union with the wash. In the white and well-lit stillroom gleam two high stills, one wash, one spirit, each with one 'onion' and straight, wide swan necks allowing up to eight refluxes, and therefore a lighter spirit. A brand-new spirit safe inscribed 'Abercrombie, May 2000' sits directly on top of the low wines and feints charger which is barrel-shaped, of varnished oak and with green hoops echoing those on the washbacks – a splendid spectacle.

Access Excellent and comprehensive – no holds barred.

Visual impact Glenkinchie presents a nice blend of factory and magic. The stillroom is particularly bright and white.

Range The range of Classic Malts and other UDV products, both malts and blends.

Style The talented designers have combined a warehouse motif with warmth, colour and light.

Staff The tour guides – perennially friendly, informative, and helpful.

Catering No facilities – some in Pencaitland. Tasty sandwiches available at the garage.

Toilets Close to reception – functional, clean and tidy. Loos for the disabled at reception.
Parent and baby – no facilities.

This has everything – huge stills, smoky kilns, that spirit safe set on its varnished plinth, and a museum which belies the image of fustiness one associates with that word. It is alive, full of fascinating insights. We loved the collection of 'dogs' which warehousemen secreted down their trouser legs after a surreptitious and highly illicit dip in a cask. The tour is excellent for the fleet of foot and the less agile alike, and the 'dram fest' at the end a fitting climax to a wow of an experience. Drink a silent toast to these super guides as you stumble forth, a shakier if a wiser person.

Overall rating

SCOTCH MALT WHISKY SOCIETY

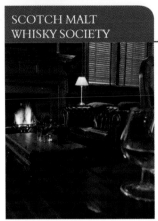

A unique establishment which caters for members who relish an ever-changing selection of top-class, cask-strength malts.

Established in 1983 by Pip Hills and some fellow malt whisky enthusiasts, the SMWS has known good times and bad but now boasts over 20,000 members worldwide. A London Members' Room is also available and The Society now has branches in the USA, Japan, Switzerland (also serving Austria), France, Italy and Benelux (also serving Germany). A new membership costs £75 per year including an introductory bottle of malt. The Vaults exude a relaxed, clubby atmosphere and the facilities include four flats for rent, the Members' Room and bar and a tasting room. The London facility is more contemporary in feel and is smaller in scale. A Swiss Members' Room has also opened in Schönenwerd.

Established 1983

Enquiries 0131 554 3451 London: 0207 831 4447 Switzerland: (+41) 628 587030

Website www.smws.com

Opening hours Edinburgh: Jan-Dec, Mon-Wed, 10am-5pm; Thu-Sat, 10am-11pm. London: Mon-Fri, 12.00-10pm (no children allowed).

Getting there At the bottom of Leith Walk, turn left along Great Junction Street and then first right into Henderson Street. The Vaults are on the right hand side after the street bends to the right.

Parking/reception Free on-street parking available. Entry via a wrought-iron gate set in a high wall at the corner of Giles Street and Henderson Street. Climb the exterior stairs above The Vintner's Room restaurant to the first-floor entrance and report to reception. As this is a members-only facility you must be the guest of a member, or be prepared to join the society when there.

Tour frequency Staff will be happy to show you around if convenient.

Maximum group size 16 for tastings, 65 for private functions in Members' Room.

Cost £25 per annum renewal.

Group bookings Available for tastings and private dining parties by appointment.

Visual aids Not applicable.

Foreign visitors Members welcome.

Photography? Ask at reception first.

Disabled access As The Vaults are a listed building, there is no disabled access. However, if the flight of external stairs can be tackled, then access is generally good and there are always helping hands available.

THE MALTS

Bond In various locations throughout Scotland. The society purchases selectively and stores stock where it is most convenient.

Casks Bottlings come from the full range of casks used in the industry.

Bottling Carried out under contract for the society. Dark green bottles with tasteful cream and green labels bearing the SMWS logo and with distillery numbers in red. Cork stoppered.

Experts' opinion The society employs a tasting panel which meets regularly to select bottlings from a range of distillers' samples. The panel is chaired by Charles MacLean and ensures that rogue casks are not allowed into the supply chain!

Our dram Now this is where you can get seriously led astray. At the bar there are any number of malts available from the stock currently being bottled. The price of a dram is usually £2.50 and the choice is therefore completely up to yourself. We tried a 2.33, which was King George IV's favourite tipple and is a classic Speyside. Drawn from a sherry butt, it was not too reminiscent of that fact. Fruity nose, with a hint of chocolate. After we added a dash of water, the fruits came to the fore but the sweetness was not as pronounced as we had expected. Full-bodied, delicious. Price for a bottle: £43 at 62.4%abv, distilled in 1986, age 14 years.

The range of cask-strength whiskies available from The Society is quite staggering. Over the years almost the entire portfolio of Scotland's distilleries (living and dead) has been represented in the SMWS bottlings. The Society cannot name the malts it bottles, but uses a simple numbering system to aid identification. This allied to the cryptic clues given in the lists, means that identification is relatively simple. At the time of going to press The Society was bottling malts from all the whisky producing regions. The Society like to deconstruct the regions a little and tend to catalogue their bottlings by region and then river source, if appropriate. This means that bottling 11.21 is classed as a Findhorn from Greater Speyside and 7.18 as a Lossie from the same area. In the Spring Bottlings 2001 brochure, we counted 23 malts on offer and two special liqueurs produced by Drambuie using an Island and a Speyside malt.

Special features Once you are a member of the SMWS a whole new range of experiences is available to you. You can arrange private tastings and entertain your fellow whisky enthusiasts, or you can attend one of the 80 or so UK-wide tastings organised by the SMWS on a regular basis. These are ticket-only events and cost around £20-25 per head. The Whisky School is run twice a year in both Edinburgh and London and costs £185/£230 for members respectively. (Non-members can also attend them at a cost of £210/£255.) There are also four flats at the Vaults which can be rented.

THE VAULTS

Style The Members' Room is the heart of The Society at its Leith headquarters. The Vaults used to be part of the firm of wine merchants, J&G Thomson Ltd, and the Members' Room was formerly the clerk's office. 'Room' is perhaps the wrong word, because it is more of a hall. Two fires burn on the far wall, comfy chairs abound and there is always space to find a corner to read the paper. Very clubby in feel, but it does not reek of 'them and us'.

Staff Great. They know their stuff and are always on hand. The bar is staffed and waitresses deal with the food orders.

Catering Light lunches at reasonable prices. The facilities can be booked for functions and private dining.

Toilets Clean and hygienic. No loo for the disabled. **Parent and baby** – no facilities.

SUMMARY

A haven for whisky lovers who appreciate the finer things in life. Beautiful surroundings and a relaxed and cosy atmosphere. A great place to sip and savour a dram or two, to meet friends, take lunch or catch up on the news. Worth considering for a private function with a whisky slant. The London facility is an altogether different experience but is proving very popular with members south of the Border. We heartily recommend membership.

Overall rating

SCOTCH WHISKY HERITAGE CENTRE

Better than the real thing? Informative and amusing with wide appeal. Ideal preparation for a visit to a real distillery.

The Royal Mile and Edinburgh Castle provide a backdrop without equal. The centre is in an old school building with a beautiful façade and its own mini-turret. The restaurant and bar are open to all, and the whole place has an invigorating, cosmopolitan buzz. The retail area is open to the public so you do not have to pay the entry fee to be able to browse the whisky-related goods that are on offer. Very well positioned for visiting other Edinburgh attractions. Not to be missed.

Established 1988

Enquiries 0131 220 0441

Website www.whisky-heritage.co.uk

Opening hours Mid-Jun to Sept, all week, 9.30am-6.30pm. Sept-mid to Jun, all week, 10.30-5.30pm. Shop open from 12.30pm on Sundays.

Getting there Find Edinburgh Castle and you have found the Centre. As you climb Castlehill it's on the left just before you get to the esplanade.

Parking/reception No dedicated parking. Castle Terrace to the rear of the building usually has some metered spaces. Climb the steps from the Terrace to the Centre. Flags, and a leaflet girl in tartan mark the entrance. Reception area is past the entrance to the shop. After paying you are soon whisked into the theatre for an excellent video

presentation and a warm welcome from your guide – as likely to be from Australia or South Africa as from Scotland.

Tour frequency On demand.

Group size 30

Cost £6.50. Senior Citizens, £4.50. 5-17 year olds, £3.25. Family ticket, £14.

Group bookings Groups and school parties welcome by appointment – special party rates available.

Visual aids Video, holograms and models – all high quality state-of-the-art stuff

Foreign visitors Commentaries in eight languages: Dutch, French, German, Italian, Spanish, Portuguese, Japanese, English – again of the highest quality.

Photography? Yes

Disabled access Excellent.

THE PRODUCT

Malts   A huge range.

Owner   Scotch Whisky Heritage Centre

Regions   All are represented.

Ages   From three to over 50 years old.

Water source The importance of water in whisky is well-illustrated in the tour.

Malting Again, the process is covered well.

Bond Plenty of illustrations of casks, their sizes and origins.

Bottling Blending is superbly illustrated by the 'Master Blender' (a hologram), nosings on tour and (at a price) in the Whisky Bar.

Experts' opinion This is the place to study, sample and buy the best of Scotch malt, blends and bottled grain whisky. If you fancy the exotic try an Ardbeg at £245, a Glenfarclas at £1500 or a real snip – a Macleans' 49 at £2000. The Centre celebrates the whole range of whiskies and the drams on the tour come from a range of blends, some of them lesser known than others.

Our dram We enjoyed a generous measure of Mackinlay's 5 year old. No need to drown this one in lemonade.

TOUR EXPERIENCE

This is not a distillery, but it feels like it. The tour is informative, beautifully illustrated, amusing, romantic and fun. Guides are very competent and able to satisfy the casual visitor and the knowledgeable. Surprisingly the odd howler survives as we were told that the River Spey principally provides cooling water and *not* process water!

Special features This is a part-tour, part-video presentation then the visit to the 'Master Blender' and, as the climax, the barrel ride. All are faultless in terms of logistics and balance. The experience begins with a dram and a 10-minute film based on an American tourist's visit to an Islay distillery. It is an excellent introduction, with a nice touch of humour and one which is sustained throughout the tour. Then the guide takes you to an illustrated talk with an opportunity to nose raw, grain and mature spirit in order to contrast them and then a chance to feel and smell real peat. Next comes a 'lightning tour' of a superb model of Tormore Distillery. The excellent information on grain distilling – a continuous process in a gigantic Coffey still – is hard to get elsewhere and reminds visitors that whisky distilling is not all about peatreek and romance. An illuminated map of the regions and a good question-and-answer session follows. The hologram of the master blender's ghost is convincing: his patter is fun and to the point, and his expertise and knowledge are well put over – nice humour again. Finally comes the journey through time on a barrel car. History can be fun when it comes like this, from medieval times to the present: the bootleggers and the VE day scenes particularly appealed. Lifelike, with aromas – perhaps just a little lacking in action and movement – but definitely in the Yorvik class. A very fine experience overall.

Access Just like many a real distillery, there are quite a lot of steps to negotiate – there are lifts for the disabled to every level.

Visual impact Nearly as good as the real thing – it's only those glorious aromas in the whisky-making process that they can't recreate.

SHOP

Range You name it – comprehensive range of malts, blends and liqueurs plus foods, confectionery, books in many languages, glasses, CDs, postcards, sweaters and teeshirts (the range could be better) pens, tea towels. First and foremost, a whisky browsers' paradise.

Style Bright, classy, pointed-arch whisky stands, tartan carpets, roof arches reminiscent of those in a mini-cathedral.

Staff Busy but helpful – impressively knowledgeable and well-versed in the requirements of the foreign visitor – and the native.

Catering On the lower ground floor, bright and white, with windows overlooking Castle Terrace. This is where you end up after the tour. On one side is the Whisky Bond Bar where you can sample, at a price, a huge array of malts and blends, the former arranged by region. For a fiver you can buy a sample tray of malts from all the producing regions. Across the way the Whisky Bond Bistro is worth visiting in its own right. Open all day with meals from 12.30pm-4.30pm, there is every kind of soft drink along with wine, beer, and beverages, coffee, really tasty sandwiches, home-made cakes and more. Note the quotations on the roof beams. We rather liked Dr. Samuel Johnson's excuse for taking a dram – 'To let me know what it is that makes a Scotchman happy.'

Toilets Well-used, acceptable, clean – arguably have slipped a bit since they won an award! Disabled toilets – good, clean provision. **Parent and baby** – excellent: located in the disabled toilet at restaurant level.

SUMMARY

Informative and amusing with a wide appeal for both the casual visitor and children as well as those with a genuine interest. The Centre is worth a visit in its own right and should engender a desire to visit a distillery as well. You even take home a certificate to prove you have 'done' the tour – a nice parting touch – just the thing to frame beside my certificate of competence to drive a tractor but based on rather better evidence.

Overall rating

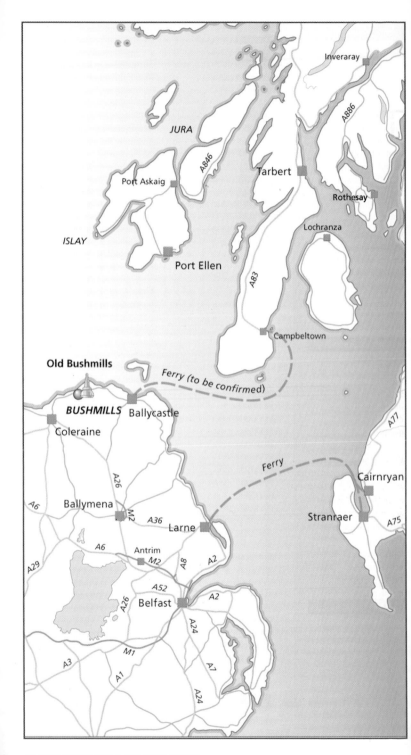

Northern Ireland

TOURING CENTRE: BUSHMILLS

The only working distillery visitor centre in Ireland is at Bushmills, in Northern Ireland, close to the Antrim Coast and the Giant's Causeway. If you are looking to combine a visit there with other whisky-related activities, there are two obvious options, both of which call for a bit of travelling.

One is to head south to visit Irish Distillers' site 12 miles (19km) east of Cork where the old 18th-century Midleton Distillery has been turned into the Jameson Heritage Centre. Visitors can see the 'largest pot still in the world' and the old waterwheel together with various historic and architecturally unique buildings. There is a dram at the end of the tour.

Opening Times: Mar-Oct, Mon-Sun, 10am-6pm (last tour 4.30pm); Nov-Feb, Mon-Fri, tours at 12pm and 3pm; Sat & Sun, 2pm and 4pm. Tel: 021 463 1821. (From the UK dial 00353 21 then the last seven digits.)

Another option is the Old Jameson Distillery in Smithfield, Dublin. This is not a living distillery but there is a marvellous audio-visual display, a tour of the old distillery, and a tasting. The catering is very good and the sheer scale of the facility gives you an idea of just how large the distillery must have been at the height of its powers during the Victorian era. At one point on the tour you can actually walk into the brick furnace structure on top of which a pot still once rested. The size of this is a little difficult to imagine until experienced at first hand.

Opening Times: All year, 9.30am-6pm, (last tour at 5pm). Tel: 01 807 2355. (From the UK dial 00353 1 then the last seven digits.)

While visiting Bushmills, drop in to the Bushmills Inn (028 2073 2339) – renowned for its food. It's a bit pricey but good. The Ramore Restaurant and Wine Bar at Portrush (the wine bar provides excellent family food at £8-9 per head) is also worth a try. Cromore Halt at Port Stewart has accommodation and a restaurant. It is a really good and inexpensive place for b&b where you can indulge in some hearty trenching.

Other places to visit are the Giant's Causeway where the visitor centre echoes the twin pagodas of Bushmills, the fortress at Dunluce, and the Carrick-a-Rede rope bridge once used by salmon fishermen and now a major tourist attraction for those untroubled by vertigo. The Antrim coast is a also a golfers' paradise and a trout fisherman's dream.

Oldest licensed distillery in the world and still the best – in Ireland at least!

The buildings at Bushmills are a nice blend of the old and the new, with most post-dating a disastrous fire in 1885 which left only the grain store unscathed. Bushmills is a picture of weathered stone and tile, with rich-red wood and walls freshly whitewashed. The dam holding the precious water from St. Columb's Rill is beautifully set, the inspiration for countless watercolours and postcards. While the town of Bushmills may not be the prettiest in Antrim, the distillery more than compensates – and the creature comforts add to the allure. Best way to get there is by the restored electric tramway from the coast with dramatic vistas of sands and river – being in Ireland the trams are horse-drawn!

Established 1608

Enquiries 028 2073 1521

Website www.irish-whiskey-trad.com

Opening hours Apr-Oct, Mon-Sat, 9am-5.30pm; Sun, 12-5.30pm; Nov-Mar, Mon-Fri, 9am-4.30pm. Five tours in the winter.

Getting there An easy hour and a bit from Aldergrove Airport on the B66. The distillery is on the right. The Antrim Coast Road from Larne is more picturesque: head inland near the Giant's Causeway.

Parking/reception Ample parking on the left as you enter. Reception exudes warmth to match the welcoming smiles on the cheery faces of Valerie and her team: it makes buying a ticket a positive pleasure. The entrance is on your left as you approach the distillery from the car park.

Tour frequency Summer as required. Winter: five tours at 10.30am, 11.30am,

1.30pm, 2.30pm and 3.30pm 'sharp'.

Maximum group size 30

Cost £3.95.

Group bookings Please telephone to arrange visits.

Visual aids An excellent video starts the tour, shown in the Cooperage Theatre – pretty pictures, nice images, especially of the prohibition era, pride in history and heritage and the softest of sells. Could be clearer on the distilling process.

Foreign visitors Brochures in French, German, Italian & Spanish. Video by arrangement in French, Dutch, German, Italian, Spanish and Japanese. Summer guides have European languages.

Photography in distillery? No

Disabled access The tour is daunting with many steps and levels. Access is possible to reception, theatre, dram room, restaurant and to warehouse.

THE PRODUCT

Malt Bushmills

Owner Irish Distillers Group plc

Region Northern Ireland

Ages 10, 12, 16 (double-matured in Port) & 21 years old (double-matured in Madeira)

Water source From St. Columb's Rill which flows over basalt as at the Giant's Causeway.

Malting Optic, Chariot and now Fractol varieties grown mainly in Co Kildare, and malted at Cork with no peat.

Bond Six warehouses on site. In the one we visited 7,000 barrels are stored in ten racks on a concrete floor. A raised gallery gives splendid

views and a heady whiff of the angel's share.

Casks Ex-bourbon and a few sherry. Port and Madeira for the double-matured.

Bottling On site. Look out for Jameson as well as Bushmills. 180 bottles per minute.

Experts' opinion The ten year old, matured in bourbon casks has a warm sweetness, overtones of vanilla and a long peat-free malty aftertaste.

Our dram Thrusting aside a betrayal of our Scottish roots, we both opted for the 12-year-old Bushmills (sold only on site) which the guide advises should be allowed to linger on the tongue. We did this to good effect, – smooth, velvety, spicy and fruity. We left with a bottle in the sporran.

Above-average tour: guides are friendly, approachable, and welcome questions. Groups can be largish, but there is space. On-site videos at the mashtun and bottling plant are excellent and there are microphones for the guide at all key points. The pace is fairly brisk, but somehow you feel unhurried. Distillery staff join in to answer questions and contribute to the 'family' feel. More could be made of milling and how the stills undergo triple distillation takes a bit of grasping.

Special features Little is shown of the milling process but the magnificent mashtun more than compensates. Although only 28 years old, it was made in cast-iron sections bolted together and is painted maroon. It boasts a sparkling, handsome brass rim, and an elegant burnished copper canopy. It has a capacity of 43,000 litres (9,470 gallons) and each mash takes six and a half hours. The 'wet grains' (draff) goes for cattle feed. Then on to the washbacks in an immaculate room in sober industrial grey, well-lit and airy. There are ten stainless steel washbacks into which yeast is fed from a 'bub-tub'. They are a bit short on the warmth so prevalent elsewhere at Bushmills. The still-room is approached from on high and wins the 'best stillroom aroma' award by miles. All seven stills are elegant, fairly tall and slender, with narrow lyne arms extending to copper condensers which are as highly lacquered as the stills themselves. The two with red embossed shields are wash stills, raising the spirit strength from about 7% abv to 25% abv, and the other five are spirit stills which are charged with spirit in two further distillations which raises the alcoholic strength to 70% abv and then 85% abv. Triple distillation and unpeated kilning of the barley gives Bushmills its distinctive smooth characteristics. Perhaps it is the complexity of all this which leads to rather more pipes and plant obscuring the views of the stills than elsewhere, and this is frustrating as these stills are very handsome indeed. The warehouse visit is worthwhile, and the visit to the bottling plant is a unique and spectacular climax to the tour – at Glenfiddich you see the bottles, at Bushmills you hear them as well! The tasting experience was fun and takes place in the dram room beside the distillery kitchen. Visitors can sample any of the malts and blends, coffee or soft drinks, or, joy of winter joys, a hot toddy with cinnamon. If 'volunteers' are sought during the tour, get in quick – it can lead to an organised tasting of blends and malts, with Scotch examples as a comparison. You have to plump for the best blend, which was Powers for us, and the best malt.

Access Excellent – bright airy, well-lit with good views and broad stairs.

Visual impact Spick and span and clearly loved. Traditional/modern blend. Stills are a bit cluttered so viewing is difficult.

Range Whiskeys from Bushmills, Jameson and Powers, both malt and blends. High-class clothing, fleeces, jumpers, golf wear, Baleek china, Tyrone glass, pictures, hats, candles and the usual array of mugs, glasses and keyrings.

Style A two-in-one shop with a wide range of whiskeys in an annexe close to the main shop. While a little cluttered, the latter, in warm green and wood texture, has attractive displays and enticing corners.

Staff This is Ireland! A friendly, helpful, 'extra-mile' approach.

Catering The Distillery Kitchen is spacious in green and pine with a distinctly farmhouse feel. The home-made scones and the delectable wheaten bread strengthened that impression. Come lunchtime the talented Liz and her staff conjure up a tasty range of goodies ranging from soup and toasties to shepherd's pie and salads. The ploughman's lunch is hard to beat. Wines augment the usual range of drinks and refreshments. Highly recommended.

Bushmills exudes warmth and character. If it was the only distillery you were to visit, it would be ideal. The tour is excellent, the visual impact is good, the home-made food irresistible. The shop is stocked with discernment and the enthusiasm of the staff is infectious. Combine it with excursions to the Giant's Causeway and the ancient fortress of Dunluce, and you are in the realms of superlatives. As a visitor experience, and for a good dram, it is up with the best Scotland can offer. And perhaps it should be thus ... after all, were the secrets of usquebaugh not first passed from Irish monks to the Gaels of the Hebridean isles?

Overall rating

abv Alcohol by volume, expressed as a percentage.

Aftershots See *feints*.

Age The age given on any bottling of whisky, be it *single malt*, *vatted malt* or a *blend* will be the age of the youngest constituent whisky.

Alcohol The by-product which accumulates during *fermentation*. The process of *distillation* produces greater concentrations of alcohol.

Ageing See *maturation*.

Angels' share The term used to describe the evaporation of alcohol lost to the atmosphere from maturing whisky stocks. Usually about 2% per annum.

Blend A blended Scotch whisky is a mix of neutral *grain whisky* and malt whiskies. Commonly a proprietary *blend* will contain 25% malt whiskies and 75% *grain whisky*. Around 90% of all whisky sold is blended, and 10% is *single malt*.

Bond The term for the warehouse in which maturing stocks of whisky are stored for a minimum of three years. After excise duty is levied and paid, the whisky can be removed for bottling.

Carbon dioxide The gas which is created when *fermentation* takes place.

Cask strength The strength of a whisky when it leaves the cask after maturation. It can be as high as 60% abv and is normally reduced to 40 or 43% for bottling.

Casking See *fillings*.

Chill filtration The process of chilling and filtering whisky before bottling which removes the fatty acids that lead to 'clouding' of the bottled product in low temperatures. Aficionados claim that some taste is removed at the same time.

Coffey still The distilling apparatus patented by Aeneas Coffey in 1830 which allowed the continuous *distillation* of *wash* made from a variety of cereals. The product is very pure *alcohol* of high strength lacking in many of the components found in a *pot still* whisky. The modern equivalent is called the *patent* or *continuous still*.

Condenser The apparatus which cools the hot alcoholic vapours emanating from the *lyne arm* into liquid spirit.

Continuous still See *Coffey still*.

Cooperage The craft of manufacturing and maintaining casks and barrels.

Coppers The other name for the hot water tanks supplying the mashtun.

Coup A receptacle containing a measured amount of *grist* prior to being mixed in the *mashtun* with hot water.

Dipstick The stick-like instrument used to 'dip' and measure the contents of the *spirit receiver*. Try to sniff it after use!

Distillation The process whereby *alcohol* is produced from *wash* in copper *pot stills*. *Alcohol* has a lower boiling point than water and is therefore driven off sooner and then collected in the *condenser*. In the manufacture of *grain whisky*, this process is continuous and is carried out in a *patent* or *continuous still*.

Draff The residue left in the *mashtun* after the dissolved sugars have been extracted and the *wort* drained off. It is used as a food for livestock. See also *wet grains*.

Dram The Gaelic for a large drink. Commonly applied to a generous measure of Scotch whisky.

Feints Also known as *tails* or *aftershots*. This is the final part of the spirit *run* through the *spirit safe* during *distillation*. This portion of the *run* is then re-distilled.

Fermentation The process which takes place in the *washbacks* whereby a low-strength alcoholic beer and *carbon dioxide* are produced after *yeast* is introduced to the *worts*.

Fillings The name for spirit which has come from the *spirit receiver* and is used to fill casks in the filling store.

Foreshots Also known as *heads*, this is the initial part of the spirit *run* through the *spirit safe*. High in *alcohol*, up to 80% *abv* and volatile impurities. Diverted to the intermediate *spirit receiver* and re-distilled.

Floor maltings The stone floors on which traditional *malting* takes place. Now only seen in action in a handful of places such as the most northerly distillery at Highland Park, Orkney and almost the most southerly at Springbank in Campbeltown.

Gauger The old name for an exciseman employed to combat smuggling in the 18th and 19th centuries.

Grain whisky Whisky that has been produced in a *continuous still* from a cereal *mash* of wheat or maize. Output is used in blended Scotch.

Green malt The name given to barley that is ready for *kilning* after having lain on the malting floors to allow germination.

Grist The malted barley that has been ground in a roller mill to a specified consistency prior to mashing.

Heads See *foreshots*

Kilning The process of drying *green malt* to stop germination in order to preserve the soluble sugar content in the cereal grains. Drying in peat smoke will also affect the levels of *phenols* present in the malted barley.

Low wines The spirit produced by the first *distillation* of *wash* in the *wash still*. This has a strength of about 21% *abv*.

Low wines still See *spirit still*.

Lyne arm The part of the still connecting the head, or neck of the still to the *condenser*. The dimensions and the angle of slope to the *condenser* can vary enormously.

Malt The common name for barley after it has gone through the *malting* process.

Malting The process of controlled germination and then the drying of barley to preserve sugar content for *fermentation*.

Maltings Where the industrial *malting* of barley takes place. Most barley produced nowadays is made in these large plants. See also *floor maltings*.

Marrying In blended Scotch, this means the mixing of a number of grain and malt whiskies to create a whole. In malt whisky, it is the process of mixing the same whisky (which can be of different ages) from a number of different casks. In *vatted malt* whisky, it means the mixing of a number of different malt whiskies. Again, these can be of varying ages.

Mash The porridge-like mixture of *grist* and hot water which is mixed in the *mashtun*. The liquid drained from the process is called the *wort* which is then ready for *fermentation*.

Mashtun The large metal vessel in which *grist* and hot water are mixed to produce *wort*.

Maturation The process which occurs when spirit stored in oak casks is left to age in a bonded warehouse. Also known as *ageing*.

Middle cut The central part of the spirit *run* through the *spirit safe* which is diverted to the *spirit receiver* for fillings. Depending on temperature, it has a strength of about 67% abv and is relatively free from impurities present in the *feints* and *foreshots*.

Milling The process of grinding malted barley to produce *grist*.

Nose The aroma and bouquet of a whisky. A key indicator for a master blender when creating blends.

Pagoda The characteristically shaped roof and smoke outlet of a traditional Scottish malt kiln. Design attributed to the distillery architect Charles Doig in the 1880s.

Patent still See *Coffey still*

Peat Compacted vegetable matter found in large bogs and mosses which, after being cut into sods, is commonly used as a domestic fuel. It is used as a secondary (and sometimes primary) drying agent in the process of *kilning*.

Peated malt Malt which has been wholly or partly dried over a *peat* heat source during *kilning*.

Phenols Hydroxyl derivatives of aromatic hydrocarbons which are produced when *kilning green malt* in *peat* smoke and are responsible for the peaty characteristics of many malt whiskies.

Pot ale The high-protein residue left in the *wash still* after *distillation* and which is sometimes mixed with *draff* to make cattle cake.

Pot still The traditional onion-shaped copper vessel used in the process of *distillation* in malt whisky distilleries. In Ireland it is still used to produce traditional pot still Irish whiskey.

Reflux This occurs when alcoholic vapour, having risen to the neck the still, falls back to be redistilled. Some stills such as at Dalmore and Fettercairn have water-cooled jackets to encourage this. Ardbeg has a reflux pipe to aid the process.

Rummager The rotating chain inside direct-fired stills that prevents solids sticking to the bottom.

Run The name given to the colourless distilled spirit as it passes through the *spirit safe*.

Silent season The period each year when a distillery closes for maintenance, repairs to stills etc. Visitors miss out on smells and aromas but can often get to see much more at close hand.

Single malt The malt whisky product of a single distillery.

Spent lees The residue from the second *distillation* in the *spirit still*. The only waste-product of the whole distilling process.

Spirit receiver The receptacle for distilled spirit collected prior to casking.

Spirit safe A brass-bound and glass-fronted case through which spirit flows as it comes from the stills. Specific gravity and alcoholic strength are checked here.

Spirit still Where the *distillation* of *low wines* takes place. The *spirit still* is commonly smaller than the *wash still*. Also known as the *low wines* still.

Steep The tank in which barley is steeped in water before being made into *green malt*.

Stillhouse/stillroom The part of the distillery where *distillation* takes place and which houses the *wash stills*, *spirit stills* *condensers*, *spirit safe* and *spirit receiver*.

Tails See *Feints*

Uisge beatha Gaelic for 'water of life'. 'Uisge' was eventually corrupted to 'whisky'. The Irish equivalent is 'usque-baugh'.

Underback The vessel in which *wort* from the *mashtun* is held prior to transferral via the *wort* coolers to the *washbacks* for *fermentation*.

Vatted malt A bottled whisky made from malt whiskies from more than one distillery.

Wash The mixture of *wort* and *yeast* in the *washback* which produces a low-strength alcoholic beer prior to *distillation* in the *wash still*.

Washback The vessel in which *fermentation* takes place. May be made of Scottish larch, Oregon pine or stainless steel.

Wash still The vessel in which the *distillation* of *wash* takes place. Commonly larger than the *spirit still*. The *low wines* produced in the *wash still* are then re-distilled in the spirit or *low wines* still.

Wet grains The name given to *draff* in Ireland.

Worm The name given to the coiled copper tubing which runs from the *lyne arm*. It is suspended in the cooling water held in the *worm tub*.

Wort The sweet-tasting sugary liquor produced during the mashing process (see also *mash*) which is cooled and then mixed in the *washbacks* with *yeast* and allowed to ferment.

Worm tub The traditional type of *condenser* consisting of a large cooling vat of running water through which the *worm* passes. Can be witnessed in operation at Dalwhinnie and Talisker.

Yeast A living micro-organism essential for the process of *fermentation*. Feeding on the sugar released during mashing and present in the *wort*, it produces *alcohol* and *carbon dioxide*.

If you have recently visited a distillery and would like us to know how your visit went, please complete the form below (or photocopy it) and send it to **FREEPOST NWP** (no stamp required within the UK). Alternatively, you can fax it us on **0141-221-5363** or log on to **www.visitingdistilleries.com** and complete the form online. In doing so you will be helping us to keep the guide as up to date and as accurate as possible.

PERSONAL DETAILS

Name ....

Address ....

....

City ....

County ....

Zip/Postcode ....

Country ....

e-mail address ....

COMMENTS

Distillery: .... Date of visit: ....

What was the quality of your tour like?

....

....

....

How did you find the setting and ambience of the distillery?

....

....

....

What did you think of the catering (if applicable)?

....

....

....

And the toilet facilities?

....

....

....

Finally, how did you enjoy your dram!

....

....

....

Any other comments you would like to make?

....

....

....

....

....

....

Thank you

Duncan and Wendy Graham.

DATA PROTECTION ACT 1998

Your personal details submitted on this form and provided by or collected from you in future will be held by Neil Wilson Publishing Ltd ('NWP') on electronic media and may be used by NWP to inform you (by post and/or e-mail) of forthcoming publications from NWP. If you do not want your details to be held in this manner and do not want to receive further information, please tick this box. ☐

By submitting these details, you acknowledge that you have read and understood the above section entitled 'DATA PROTECTION ACT 1998' and consent to the use described in that section.